Who's on First?

PHOENIX POETS

LLOYD SCHWARTZ

Who's on First?

New and Selected Poems

THE UNIVERSITY OF CHICAGO PRESS

Chicago and London

The University of Chicago Press, Chicago 60637
The University of Chicago Press, Ltd., London
© 2021 by The University of Chicago
Published 2021
Printed in the United States of America

30 29 28 27 26 25 24 23 22 21   1 2 3 4 5

ISBN-13: 978-0-226-79508-9 (paper)
ISBN-13: 978-0-226-79511-9 (e-book)
DOI: https://doi.org/10.7208/chicago/9780226795119.001.0001

Library of Congress Cataloging-in-Publication Data

Names: Schwartz, Lloyd, 1941- author.
Title: Who's on first? : new and selected poems / Lloyd Schwartz.
Other titles: Phoenix poets.
Description: Chicago ; London : The University of Chicago Press, 2021. |
    Series: Phoenix poets
Identifiers: LCCN 2021058781 | ISBN 9780226795089 (paperback) | ISBN
    9780226795119 (ebook)
Subjects: LCGFT: Poetry.
Classification: LCC PS3569.C5667 W46 2021 | DDC 811/.54—dc23
LC record available at https://lccn.loc.gov/2021058781

♾ This paper meets the requirements of ANSI/NISO Z39.48-1992
(Permanence of Paper).

CONTENTS

ACKNOWLEDGMENTS

The author gratefully acknowledges the editors of the following publications, in print and online, in which the new poems in this volume first appeared:

> *Golden Streetcar*: "The World"
> *Harvard Review*: "Vermeer's Pearl," "Escher: *Still Life with Mirror (1934)*," and "Lubitsch's *Angel*"
> *Plume*: "God Hour" and "The Rehearsal"
> *Poem-a-Day* (The Academy of American Poets): "In Emily Dickinson's Bedroom"
> *Salamander*: "My Doctor's Death"
> *Salmagundi*: "Harvest" and "Ralph Hamilton's Faces"

The poems from *These People* were first published in book form by Wesleyan University Press in 1981.

"Titian's *Marsyas*" was first published in *The Eloquent Poem: 128 Poems and Their Making*, ed. Elise Paschen (New York: Persea Books, 2019).

"Astronomer" was first published in *The Plume Anthology of Poetry*, volume 5, ed. Daniel Lawless (Cheshire, MA: MadHat Press, 2017).

Special thanks to the editors of the Best American Poetry series, *The Best of the Best American Poetry*, the Pushcart Prize, and *Poetry Daily* for reprinting a number of poems in this volume. To Frank Bidart and Tara Skurtu for the care and thoughtfulness with which they read and reread the manuscript for this book. And to Randolph Petilos for all his work on behalf of the Phoenix Poets series.

from These People (1981)

WHO'S ON FIRST?

"You can be so inconsiderate."

                              "You are too sensitive."

"Then why don't you take my feelings into consideration?"

                                             "If you
weren't so sensitive, it wouldn't matter."

                              *

"You seem to care about me only when you want me to do something
for you."

          "You do too much for people."

                              *

"I thought you were going home because you were too tired to go with me
to a bar."

          "I was. But Norman didn't want to come here alone."

                              *

"I'm awfully tired. Do you mind taking the subway home?"

                                             (Silence.)

"You could stay over . . ."

                    (Silence.)

"I'll take you home."

                    (Silence.)

                              *

"Why do we have sex only when you want to?"

                                   "Because you want to have sex
all the time."

                              *

"Relationships work when two people equally desire to give to each other."

"Relationships rarely work."

*

"Do you love me?"

"Of course—; but I resent it."

*

"Why aren't you more affectionate?"

"I am."

*

"Couldn't we ever speak to each other without irony?"

"Sure."

*

"I love you, you know."

"Yes . . . but why?"

*

"Do you resent my advice?"

"Yes. Especially because you're usually right."

*

"Why do you like these paintings?"

"What isn't there is more important than what is."

*

"Your taste sometimes seems strange to me."

                              "I'm a Philistine."

"A real Philistine would never admit it."

                         "I suppose you're right."

                    *

"Aren't you interested in what I care about?"

                         "Yes. But not now."

                    *

"We should be more open with each other."

                                   "Yes."

"Shall we talk things over?"

                    "What is there to say?"

                    *

"Are you ever going to cut down on your smoking?"

                              "It's all right—I
don't inhale."

                    *

"Sometimes I get very annoyed with you."

                         "The world is annoying."

                    *

"Your cynicism is too easy."

                    "Words interfere with the expression
of complex realities."

                    *

"Do you enjoy suffering?"

                              "You can't work if you don't suffer."

"But we suffer anyway."

                 "I know."

*

"Do you think we ever learn anything?"

                                  "I've learned to

do without."

*

"You're always so negative."

                     "I feel death all the time."

"Are you afraid of anything?"

                       "Not working."

*

"What shall we do for dinner?"

                            "It doesn't matter—whatever you'd like."

*

"Why don't you care more?"

                     "I do."

HANNAH

I walk on hooked rugs; my beds are covered with
patchwork. Across the road they sell
corn and red beans—fresh picked,
and the milk in bottles has a layer of cream
an inch thick at the top. This was my father's home
I have come back to. My elderly cousin
is working her latest jig-saw puzzle in the spare room.
My guest for the weekend is a young teacher,
with hair longer than mine, and a nicely trimmed
beard; he is reading my first editions.
We'll talk about novels and politics, read the papers,
play Scrabble with my elderly cousin, catch up on
the unread magazines. He'll help me carry and unload
the books I have moved here from the city; steel-wool
the old chest, ready for refinishing.
So many complicated, trivial, and
lovely things. A sturdy old leather bible, with gold edges,
and patterns in the rough grain, the names of ancestors
firmly inscribed. I have had a good life,
without sex, or sordidness, or unmerited happiness.

MUG SHOTS

"Black?"
        "Yes."
                "How many?"
                        "Three."
                                "How old?"
"Young—twenty. Big guys."
                        "Call that
young? They've been out on the streets for
years, probably. Did they show a weapon?"

"No, just surrounded me. They were coming
down the other side of the street while I was
getting out of my car, and suddenly—
I'm surrounded. Tore my pants pocket right off!"

"You were lucky. Some guys get cut up . . .
pretty bad."
                "Lucky I didn't have much on me."

"Guy with his girlfriend in the park, sleeping
peacefully in the sun—people all around. Wakes up,
there's a knife up against his throat.

Guy says he wants money for drugs, says: 'Don't move,
or I'll slit your fuckin' throat. I want every-
thing you got—*I don't care what happens to me.*'

He'da been dead before anyone could've helped.

. . . Think you could spot one?"

He pulls out three photo albums. The pictures
look like the ones you get in a booth for a
quarter, only bigger.
                    All the same poses—
full face; profile. Ten or twelve to a page.

Hundreds of pages.

More "real" than a high school yearbook, or
family album . . . The pictures
don't run together. The identical poses
exaggerate the idiosyncrasies:

faces round, or sunken; hair slicked down,
or fuzzy, or limp; skin very dark, or
almost white . . .
                    One has an earring and a
blond wig; one has hardly any teeth; one has
a long, deep scar.
                    A lot aren't wearing shirts . . .
Naked? Dangerous?

"You can stop when you get tired."

Their expressions are unusually clear:
scared, or cynical; alert, or spaced out.
One looks ashamed; another is crying;
one's grinning.
                    One looks "intelligent."

—Which ones are guilty?

They all look tired . . . and guilty.

I close the book. A thin young man comes in.
"White or black?" "Black." "How old?" "Early teens."
They hand him a set of albums. I start to leave.

"Any weapons?" "A knife . . . They pulled a knife on me."
I reach into my pocket. No weapon; only
keys. Is my car still there?

I get up. I feel dizzy, and numb; my eyes ache.
—In an album I hadn't noticed, I see

my picture . . .

full face, profile; black and white.
I look nervous, "intelligent," ashamed;
I'm not wearing a shirt . . .

Shoplifting? tax evasion? defamation of character?
reckless driving? disturbing the peace? possession of
narcotics? indecent exposure? fraud?

It's too dark to see.

—I go out; it's daylight. I look around; the street
is empty . . . I walk to my car,
looking both ways, before I cross the street.

A PHILOSOPHICAL PROBLEM

"Hello?"
            "Oh, hi."

"I'm sorry, did I wake you?"
                                    "No, but I
can't talk now . . . There's someone here."

"I'm sorry. I'd like to talk to you. Can I
call you back later?"
                            "I don't think so.
Let me call you tomorrow."

"All right . . . all right. I'm afraid I've
done something foolish."
                                "Let's
talk about it tomorrow. I'll call you. G'night."

"Good night."

Please don't be upset. I feel fine today.
Really. I'd like to explain to you
what happened last night.
I had to *hurt* myself. Can you understand?
Not kill myself. I knew almost three years ago
I would do this, sooner or later.
The analysts don't help you—
they only teach you how to play.
Of *course* it's my mother's fault

for not wanting to touch me;
for divorcing my father; for
neither of them wanting to take me . . .
How could I *not* feel worthless?
How could I justify my existing?

But how can anyone—
whatever their parents were like? My problem
was not psychological; it is philosophical.
What right has *anyone* to be here?

Of course I lied to my analyst—I told her
I was depressed. She said you
can't *make* people love you;
you can't make someone even *like* you . . .
I've learned. I tried
not to tell you how much I cared, not to
force myself on you; and then I had to . . .

But all along, I had the feeling that only
pain—actual, physical pain—
would relieve my depression.

Of course, you told me I
didn't love you. How could I
when we knew each other so little?
when our "encounters" were so unsuccessful,
especially for me . . . It was true.
But I didn't believe you. I admit, now I can see
you were right: it wasn't you,
but my conviction, my fantasy
of our endless, undiluted bliss . . . You say

it could have been anyone—
if *you* were not the first person I met here,
I would have latched on to someone else.
I'm sorry it was you.
—I won't bother you again. I don't even
want to see you now; frankly,
I don't even like you anymore . . .

Maybe this still sounds crazy, but I think
if you—or someone—could have
only *touched* me last night (I don't mean sex, just
some physical contact),
I don't think I would have done it.

I hope this doesn't sound like
blackmail. Believe me, I don't mean it to!
I do know what I need.
And I was sure I wouldn't kill myself . . .

All week I felt driven. I went
to a concert alone
and couldn't stand being stuck in my seat.
I was even rude to another friend who
insisted I go with him for a drink . . . And then
running into you last night, and your sweet offer
to drive me to the subway; and your look
of *boredom*
when I finally told you how I felt about you—;
I panicked. I went straight home and took
three sleeping pills, and a glass of wine.
It only got worse; I
couldn't get the panic out of my system.

It was not crazy—though you'll probably
think it was; I knew
just what I needed to do . . . I used a pair
of very blunt scissors;
a two-by-four would have been sharper.
I knew I wouldn't kill myself.
It was very messy. I'm sorry;
but it worked . . . I knew it would work.

THE WANDERER

I'm talking about what isn't there anymore,
the *past*—"Ultimate Nostalgia"—a dead end.

I had two friends. Married. I thought they were
my best friends—the both of them; for five,
six years.
                    And I don't know, they didn't call
me, I didn't call them . . . It's been since February—
over three months. I can't even tell them
I'm leaving; what's the use?
                                        Maybe I'll
write to them. Maybe I'll call them
when I come back,—*if* I come back.
                                        I'm starting
to get too attached to city life anyway!
It's no good to be dependent on *anything*,
even a city . . .
                    "CONSTRUCTIVE NIHILISM."

I think I'm getting cynical!
                            But what happened?
We *liked* each other. Maybe we liked each other
too much; maybe they got scared . . .
                                        I thought
six years would make us "inseparable." I guess
we didn't know each other as much as we thought.

—Maybe I'm too romantic.

       Why else would
I be going out into the woods?

        The only thing
I'm going to worry about now is if there's enough
room in my pack for my books . . .

         You know what
I'm taking? Whitman, Baudelaire, and the
Arabian Nights,—right?

         Whitman is for
wandering—or sitting by the ocean,
in my tent, reading "Out of the Cradle
Endlessly Rocking." And every night, one
of the *Arabian Nights* . . .

        Baudelaire is probably
too much; that's the first book I leave behind.

—I'm planning to shed my possessions as I go.
That's *all* I'm planning.

       I have three shirts,
four pairs of socks . . . that's one pair too many,
but I suppose you can't throw good clothes away.

Possessions are ridiculous!

       It's what I'm
trying to get away from . . .

       And even now,
I can't: I've got this *tent*, and this *knife*,
and this fucking *backpack*, where I have to keep
my fucking *underwear*—

      there's no escape.

But anything will be better than this city,
which I don't even want to remember;
—which is going to explode any second,
anyway . . . I don't want to be around to
hear it.

      I'm an Anarchist,—but I'm
a *socialist* Anarchist: Socialist;
Anarchist; Existentialist . . .

                        It makes sense.
Think about it: *Existentialism*
is what you believe; *Anarchy* is what
you do, right? We're all *alone*, right? And we act
alone.

      But you can still do things for
other people—that's where the *Socialism*
comes in. It makes sense!

                  But I don't know . . . I'm
not sure *what* I believe anymore. All I know is
I talk too much;

            —and I've got to get away.

I feel nervous about going. I've never done
anything so completely on my own . . .

                    I'm nervous
about hitching, too. What if the cops
pick me up with this grass on me? I've heard
of guys being stripped by some sadist cop
who shoves his hand under your balls, or
up your ass, looking for—god knows what—"Illegal
Stimulants."

        Maybe I should get rid of
the grass.

But the whole point is to be
in my tent—*mellow*—by the sea, reading
"Out of the Cradle Endlessly Rocking."
High Noon—any time of the day! A little
loving, a little smoke, some good words . . .

I believe in loving,
                    not *love*—"The Golden Chain."
Listen, my mother just left my father
after twenty-eight years, and still lives
in the same apartment house.
                              Why did she split?
Why bother? They never talked to each other
anyway. None of us ever talked.
I was pretty close with my father, but
we never *said* anything.
                          I have four
brothers, and they're all a little crazy;
—look at *me*!
                It's not a coincidence.

"The Bonds of Matrimony" . . . I hope
I never have to get married.
                          —See this?
I can't even remember where I got it.
It's gold. Someone gave it to me . . .
                              I guess
I remember. It was a guy who liked me—
he made it. A hippie goldsmith . . . I liked
him, too.
          It couldn't have worked; he wanted
to live with me . . .
                    I'm going to give it to my
first future infatuation, the first new girl

I leave: "My darling (what was your name?), this
is for you to remember me by . . . So long!"

Nothing to lose but my chain!
                              —One less to carry.

I could write a good poem about that;
or a *novel* . . . MY LIFE & LOVES.
                              You know that poem,
"They flee from me who sometimes did me seek"?
—Sir Thomas Wyatt. He knew what he was
talking about.
                    Or maybe *I flee from them* . . .
Both; it's about the same.
                         Or Shakespeare: "Farewell,
thou art too dear for my possessing . . ."
                                   They knew.

I don't think a good poem has been written
in a hundred years.
                    What the hell do I care
about some broad's period? or some guy's
fucking hard-on? All these fucking ego trips
and masturbation fantasies.
                         Or else
anemic iambic pentameter academic
exercises. No one—NO ONE—writes
about important things anymore.
                              Rimbaud
did, Whitman did. Where's the Socialist-
Anarchist-Existentialist *POET*?

—I'm working on it; but I'm not there yet.

I've been writing a lot . . .
                              I always write things down;
I write *everything* down: look at these notebooks.
I kept a diary for about three years . . .
                                        I'm
trying to talk myself into leaving it.
There's no room;—why should I take it with me?
I keep re-reading it, to see if I can
find out where things went wrong: it doesn't help.

I hate my poems. They sound phony; and they
don't make sense.
                    I know what I want to say—
but it never comes out right; the words all
get stuck somewhere in my head.
                                    I know they're
in there; why is it so hard to find
the right ones?
                That's another reason to
keep moving . . . I'm bound to learn *something*.

I should call a couple of people before I leave.
A girl I worked with, a guy I met in a bar
a few months ago—we were pretty friendly;
smoked a lot . . .
                    I hate goodbyes. That's one
of the problems about leaving—they're too
easy to say; you find out how little
you feel.
            I think I won't.
                              Right now
I feel like I'm not anywhere . . . except
still maybe a little too close to home.

78's

for Frank Bidart

Breakable; heavy; clumsy; the end of a side
the middle of a movement—or phrase
(the faults are obvious); surface noise;
one opera—three albums, four inches, thirty-three sides wide . . .

But under the noise, the surface, the elegant
labels, the bright shellac—Revolutions: Szigeti,
Schnabel, Busch, Beecham, Casals, Toscanini *(new '30s disk star at sixty)*;
all their overtones—understood, amplified, at hand:

Our Master's Voices taking our breath,
revelations per minute, winding up in a living
room—turning the tables, taking off—moving, moving
faster (they make us think) than the speed of death.

THE RECITAL

He sits there, staring into the keyboard—
baggy rented tux; sagging shoulders; limp hair
nearly brushing the keys—

                        hesitating to begin.

His eyes glazed, as if he'd been up a week
on Coca Cola and pills;

                   a Coke bottle (giant-size)
half-empty at the foot of the piano bench . . .

A few Music people; secretaries from
his lab; the two poets he had studied with;
and assorted friends

                half-fill the small hall.

The recital is ambitious, demanding:
Romantic-ecstatic and jagged-Modern—sometimes
hard to tell apart in his playing;

frustrated by the almost willful refusal
of his fingers to deal with all the notes;

but riveting—certain that music has to "intend,"
and stopping at nothing

               to intend *something* . . .

Encouraging applause; a crooked, self-
deprecating bow from the waist.

Intermission is a relief.

"Amazing piano playing . . . for a physicist."
"Why does he *do* this to himself?"
                                        "He didn't
look happy . . ."
                    "What if he decides to play
the first half over again?"

Back inside, the conversational hum drops;
then grows . . .
                    Where is he? Still backstage?
Home? Dead? . . . The speculation is amused;

and dismayed.

Messages are sent; assurances returned.
Forty, fifty minutes . . . Nobody leaves;

no one is surprised.

Could he have done *anything* to
keep his suffering from the audience?

(How many in it had already
suffered with him his poems, jobs, addictions?)

Or is this his way of trying?

Sheepishly, he reappears . . . And begins.
No waiting.
                    His intensity—this time—
controlled by his intentions . . .

What does he have to go through—;
what process, *effort*, finally
allows him to go on?

And what defeats it?

He'd have a poem accepted by a national magazine,
using an image drawn from his experiments,—
only to withdraw it, out of fear he'd lose his job.

He'd change jobs. Move home.
And give up practicing; virtually
stop writing.

Then cancer . . . springing (he was sure)
from all the pills: making him go through
a surgical attempt to prolong his life . . .

He wanted time
to straighten himself out; to try to write more poems—

he had three months.

Dead before forty,
what brought him distinction

besides what already had?

      His astonishing diversity
      of unfulfilled talent;

      and the unrewarded
      diversity of his suffering.

SELF-PORTRAIT
for Ralph Hamilton

"I was sitting in her living room,
looking very hard at the painting I had given her.
I asked her for a knife, and very deliberately
cut up the canvas. She was furious;
I told her, 'I'll paint you a good one.'

—Every painting is a self-portrait.

I always
straighten the pictures on people's walls.

I live at home,
painting while my parents are away at work.
I cook their dinner. It's a compromise,
but it's the only way I can afford to work;
better to compromise
my life.
        And if I suffer—
so much the better; not
easy.

They're amazingly patient—
my mother thinks I'm a 'great artist.'
My paintings are all over the walls,
mostly piled up against the window
in the dining room. (The dining room
hasn't seen the light of day in three years.)

I read a lot, when I'm not painting,
and play the piano—badly.
I'm fascinated by words. Some of my paintings
have words in them: AWAY . . .
GET WELL. In college,
I wrote my autobiography.

I've been commissioned to do a portrait—
I've done several;
                    but I shouldn't do them,
I don't know how. Every portrait
becomes just another painting . . ."

In your self-portrait,
the blinds are open, but you are looking
away; your eyes green, and enormous.
There's a sunny street outside—
gray and black shadows cover your face; your mouth
twisted with irony, or tenderness,
refusing to speak.
You say, "It's just another painting."

—A train disappearing over a hill;
a burnt-out house; two trucks colliding
in mid-air;
                    your father; your mother; a baby;
a chair; a hand on a venetian blind . . .
"Every painting is a self-portrait."

from Goodnight, Gracie (1992)

for Ida Singer Schwartz

LEAVES

1

Every October it becomes important, no, *necessary*
to see the leaves turning, to be surrounded
by leaves turning; it's not just the symbolism,
to confront in the death of the year your death,
one blazing farewell appearance, though the irony
isn't lost on you that nature is most seductive
when it's about to die, flaunting the dazzle of its
incipient exit, an ending that at least so far
the effects of human progress (pollution, acid rain)
have not yet frightened you enough to make you believe
is real; that is, you know this ending is a deception
because of course nature is always renewing itself—
      the trees don't *die*, they just pretend,
      go out in style, and return in style: a new style.

2

Is it deliberate how far they make you go
especially if you live in the city to get far
enough away from home to see not just trees
but only trees? The boring highways, roadsigns, high
speeds, 10-axle trucks passing you as if they were
in an even greater hurry than you to look at leaves:
so you drive in terror for literal hours and it looks
like rain, or *snow*, but it's probably just clouds
(too cloudy to see any color?) and you wonder,

given the poverty of your memory, which road had the
most color last year, but it doesn't matter since
you're probably too late anyway, or too early—
    whichever road you take will be the wrong one
    and you've probably come all this way for nothing.

3

You'll be driving along depressed when suddenly
a cloud will move and the sun will muscle through
and ignite the hills. It may not last. Probably
won't last. But for a moment the whole world
comes to. Wakes up. Proves it lives. It lives—
red, yellow, orange, brown, russet, ocher, vermilion,
gold. Flame and rust. Flame and rust, the permutations
of burning. You're on fire. Your eyes are on fire.
It won't last, you don't want it to last. You
can't stand any more. But you don't want it to stop.
It's what you've come for. It's what you'll
come back for. It won't stay with you, but you'll
    remember that it felt like nothing else you've felt
    or something you've felt that also didn't last.

GISELA BRÜNING

Why should I remember now? More than 20 years . . . The Paris
       Opéra! My first trip to Europe.

       In the next box: Gisela Brüning and her handsome
       blond son. Had she sensed how lonely I was—

       or just how uncomfortable, craning
       from the back of my box to see the stage?

       ". . . Maybe you would like to join us?"

They helped me over the partition (an usherette
       outside, on guard against people
       sneaking in where they didn't belong).

Her English was good; her son's
       better . . . He'd have been 16—small for his age,
       with a tense, serious look on his pale,
       baby face; I was 24 . . .
                      "From Hamburg we are.
       My husband stays at home."

       (They resisted my attempt at German: I was
       their opportunity to practice English.)

Even from the Brünings' front-row seats, the opera was
        hard to see. *Roméo et Juliette*—

                                        singers I'd
        never heard of. The soprano, "mature" for
        Juliet, wore a hip-length blond wig.
        (At least she could sing the famous Waltz.)

Our discussions animated the intermissions. Past midnight,
        lingering near the Metro, we eventually
        decided to meet next day. Gisela
        wanted Holger to see Chartres—

        so we went to Chartres.

                        *

They embarrassed me, and I was embarrassed
        for them, these cultivated travelers turned
        tourist stereotype—

                                shouting to each other from
        opposite ends of the vaulted nave: f-stops and
        light-meters; which film; what scene to shoot.

        (One photo they'd send—a chapel with
        burning candles—came out rather well.)

        "It is good to remember such scenes," Gisela said.

                        *

We corresponded. Each air-letter had a motherly
        postscript: concerts they'd heard;
        museums she'd taken Holger to.

And the same invitation: Wouldn't I
　　　　　please visit? There was a bed for me. Plenty
　　　　　to eat. Operas. Museums. Hamburg was a
　　　　　great city: so very many fine things to do—

　　　　　please do not refuse.

　　　　　　　　　　　*

The following summer, I planned a trip to Greece—and a week
　　　　　with the Brünings. (They'd have loved to come
　　　　　with me: Gisela wanted Holger to see Greece.)

　　　　　　　　　　　*

Would I mind? Holger had written they were
　　　　　vegetarians. And sure enough:
　　　　　　　　　　　　　　sunflower seeds and
　　　　　raisins for breakfast; sunflower-seed-and-
　　　　　raisin sandwiches for lunch. Bowls of
　　　　　seeds and raisins on the table all day long.

　　　　　In the War, Gisela and her husband were forced to eat
　　　　　stray cats (if they were lucky to find any)—

　　　　　she could never eat meat again.

Herr Brüning was much older than his attractive,
　　　　　high-strung wife:
　　　　　　　　　　　　reticent, accommodating,
　　　　　avuncular (more Dutch than German?); happy to be
　　　　　so thoughtfully taken care of; "courtly."

And proud of his only son's accomplishments: first oboe
in his high school band (though too
shy to practice at home).

*

Gisela took us to the museum. She loved
       the German expressionists—recognized
       where all this luxury of color

       could lead, but loved the danger
       too, the brinksmanship.

Holger followed where she led, debating light-meters
       and floor-plans (how to get "There" from "Here").

       Gisela hardly minded contradiction from such a clever
       boy who knew his own mind (even if she was never
       completely convinced he was correct)—

       they argued like sparrows.

*

We went to the opera. One night,
       Rigoletto: arias in Italian, choruses in German;

       once, Benjamin Britten's *Ein Sommernachtstraum*—
       a midsummer night's dream of a production (all lights
       and shadows); its sublime quartet

       of awakening lovers . . .

*

She took us to the red-light district. Young men, she said,
       should know about such things (and it was
       Hamburg's most famous attraction).

Olive-drab military barriers guarded each end of one
       narrow street:
                     rows of narrow houses
       with wide, open windows; buxom women leaning down
       and out in gaudy peasant blouses (low-cut
       elastic bodices digging into fleshy chests);

       crowds of men cruising, stopping to inspect, to
       "negotiate."

We nudged and giggled, but Gisela was serious. She
       approved of this system. Men, she said,
       need to be relieved of their tensions.
                                   And at least
       these women were forced to stay clean.

Holger's outspoken, enlightened mother made him blush.

                     *

They took me to meet Holger's English teacher (his favorite).
       Distinguished, dapper, his suit meticulously
       pressed—he pressed my hand, pressed
       me to return . . .
                     But Gisela had every minute planned:

       so many interesting things for a visitor to do.

                     *

One excursion took us to Lübeck: Bach's church; Thomas Mann's
        house;
                bathing cabinets, bikinis, and naked
        children frolicking in the gray Baltic.

Was this the field trip I have the photo from? Holger in
        lederhosen, I in my brown English raincoat;
        a deserted grassy ridge.
                        We're perched on a bench,
        sitting on our crossed legs, eating—like tramps
        out of Beckett. (Gisela must have taken this picture;
        I'd forgotten she was there.)

                        *

Once, the Brünings had company: three or four
        stylishly-dressed women—old friends.

        There would never have been a war, they were
        still complaining, *if it wasn't for the Jews* . . .

        Gisela never commented on this visit.

                        *

Once before I left she asked what was my
        favorite food: she would make, she
        insisted, anything I liked.
                        I was dying for
a steak.

Was it thirty years since Gisela had prepared a steak?
        She must have cooked it over an hour (like
        cat?).
                I ate every leathery bite, while
        the Brünings munched their healthy legumes.

                        *

Gisela packed me a lunch for the train: bread and
          sweet-butter, raisins, fresh eggs.

          We shook hands warmly (she had a vigorous
          handshake: a tight squeeze, then two brisk pumps).

          When I later cracked open an egg, it was
          still soft (*Gisela!*), the entire compartment
          laughing themselves to tears at my eggy mess.

                    *

Holger's letters began to arrive at
          ever-widening intervals. He'd formed his
          own wind ensemble (photo included); was studying
          harder than ever at school.

          The last one had bad news.

Gisela had bought a car, and taught him to drive.
          They were touring; there was an accident (he
          was driving)—

          his mother had been killed.

                    *

I can't remember the house.

I see a big, old-fashioned kitchen: on the table, bowls of
          raisins and sunflower seeds. In a cramped bedroom, Holger
          sleeping soundly in the next bed,
                    just out of reach . . .

In one dream, I'm locked in an opera box—everyone
          singing a different language. Or I'm all
alone:
                    window-shopping in the red-light district . . .

Gisela trying to placate her reddish frizz; brushing
          the cornsilk strands out of Holger's eyes (his narrow,
ironic smile).
                         Herr Brüning at the breakfast table:
his pipe in his left hand—his contented,
knowing look.

There's no car. Every day we walk to the station, on our way
          to a museum—Gisela preparing us for the morning's
treasures:
                    her arms are exclamation points; her
voice shrills with excitement . . .

But the street is blank. The house is a blank.

Why can't I picture what it *looked* like? Why should this
          particular gap in my

          memory disturb me so?

IN THE MIST

On cool, damp evenings
at the end of July,

you can walk into a mist;
and the mist

seems to disappear—
from the dirt road; from

the hill; from the trees . . .
But in the full moon,

you can begin to see it again—
it gets closer,

leaving a ring of clearness
around you, as you walk down the hill

toward the house with the light
left in the window.

HOUSE HUNTING

FIRST AD. 2 fam. 10+4, 1 house off
Cambridge St., 24′ kit., 24′ master
bdrm. Low $100's.

"Fixed it all myself. Tore out some walls—
opened it all up; new tiles . . . Beautiful!
She wanted a dishwasher, I put in
a dishwasher, disposal—everything!
Beautiful!
            Thirty years we lived there . . .
                                    How's
seven o'clock?"

            A waxed black Coupe de Ville
pulls up at seven sharp; he heaves himself out
on the huge upholstered door . . .
                        Small, yet stooped—
a little human question mark.
                        His short
white summer shirt at least a size too big;
his pressed, but oily, olive gabardines
bunched under his belt . . . He pastes his few, sad,
last grey hairs straight back across his freckled,
sweaty scalp.
            (Was this the wound-up, do-it-
yourself voice on the other end of the line?)

40

She's even smaller. Not much younger (sixty?)
but in superior repair. Blonde; lipstick
and powder; a real figure moving under
the sheer white blouse and pink pants suit;
a Star of David—
        (Morelli? Could *he* be
Jewish too?)

      "We moved up the North Shore
just a year ago" (her hoarse rough voice
preceding us up the narrow hallway stairs)
"when he retired. Nice place.
                  I hated leaving.
Thirty years, did he tell you? . . . time!
                    I still
can't keep him home. He misses work—but, you know,
they don't miss him . . .
             If we stayed, it would've
killed him.
      This is the first time I've been back!"

She unlocks, and shows us in; he shows off
his handiwork: the glazed "Italian" tiles;
a dusty niche "built in for the Frigidaire."

A doll house:
      the "24′ kitchen" 's just
a showroom strip of white appliances,
partitioned by two drainpipe "columns" ("Tore
out some walls") from a playpen living room . . .

Some magazines (glossy, technical) lie strewn
on the dark green, winestained wall-to-wall;

upstairs, a home computer crowds one long
(24'?) and very narrow bedroom . . .

Four—tiny?—Chinese MIT grad students
rent; a widowed sister-in-law (they don't
say whose) "has the downstairs."

A shade is torn;
a cardboard mobile dangles motionless.

"Look what they've done!"
She's shaking. "—It's
scarcely been a year! I told him we
should've cleaned it up before we took
that ad.
I'm so ashamed. In thirty years
it's never looked like this! . . ."

Downstairs, it's worse—
a rabbit hole: low dusty ceilings; narrow
windows; soiled wallpaper; worn linoleum.

A labyrinth of shopping bags and cardboard
cartons stuffed with clothes. No place to move.

How long since anyone had looked down here? . . .

He doesn't say a word; she blots a tear;
I nearly hit my forehead ducking out.

We say we'll call to let them know. They know.

IMMED. OCCUPANCY. Excep-
tional high-ceilinged, fireplaced, lge
rms, detailed woodwork, mod. bath-
rooms, 3 new kitchens, 3 story house
plus basement & gar & parking. Make
offer. Must sell.

"I'm not in real estate; I'm a lawyer—I've
got to be careful. My parents gave me this house
when I was still in law school. Now I'm tied up
in a New York deal worth over a million;
I can't waste time here. I want to sell
this weekend.
                Why do you think I'm asking
so much less than the market value? . . ."

                                        Look
at the fluted marble mantels, those intricate
ceiling medallions (hand-carved mahogany),
the high-arched Victorian windows: our own
mansion—
          and a steal—
                        with "rental units"
and a parking lot . . . Could we scrape up
a down payment?

                  "Four rooms here, two bathrooms;
a five-room flat—three baths—upstairs; three rooms
with bath in the attic." There's even a rusty tub
down cellar.

Seven bathrooms? (What *was* this,
a monastery? Or a brothel—)
                                        The sinks
and johns look new . . . and pasted in; a lot of
broken windows, and warped frames.

                                        "Not safe?
There hasn't been a break-in since I've been here.
It's a good neighborhood—I don't know where
it gets the reputation. We've had great parties!

Don't worry about rent control. The rents
are high enough to pay your mortgage!" (He quotes
figures we like.)
                                        "—Besides, they don't control
how much you can charge for parking. No one asks,
no one complains;
                                        there's always a loophole . . .

                                        Look,
I've got another couple coming back tomorrow.
I don't want to pressure you (I *like* you), but
you want the house, you'll have to decide soon . . .

How much did you say you planned on putting down?"

He's not too keen about *our* figure; he wants
thirty percent—no waiting. He says
he'd even do the financing himself . . .

We'll have to make some calls tonight.
                                        Meanwhile,

we think we'd better do a little sleuthing . . .

At City Hall, the deed isn't registered
in a name we recognize (though a name we do
turns up on a lot of other properties—
whose house *is* this, anyway?)
                                  and last
changed hands less than two years ago (how long
did he say he lived there?).

                         The Rent Board says
the rents are *quite* controlled. Too controlled
to help us meet a mortgage? (How much would *we*
have to charge for parking?)
                         No one's reported
the recent plumbing and "improvements": why
didn't he want to raise the legal rent?
(What *isn't* "legal"?)

                    Our shady dream house . . .

                                              Good
we checked. Weren't we *right* to be suspicious?

But who could afford a dream house market rate,
no loopholes . . .
              Why can't we make those loopholes
work for us?

              We're wasting time. Where can we
get our hands on ready cash?
                         He said he
liked us—maybe he'll reconsider; that other
couple might be just as strapped . . .

                         We'll call
in the morning—
                tell him we want the house (*don't* we?)
and that we've got to find some way to work this out.

                    3

          SOMERVILLE. Solid 2 family in
          superior location. Cedar-shingled
          beauty with spacious aptmts & con-
          temporary updating, big sun deck &
          2 car garage.

"They're not speaking to me upstairs. My
stepdaughter. We haven't spoken since
the Doll died last year. They even
forgot my birthday . . . Seventy-three today—
would you believe it? *Cheers!*
                          Go on, look
around. I've got nothing to hide."

—It's oddly "tasteful" for this florid,
garrulous grandpa:
                   low-slung, plastic-covered,
blonde '50s "sectionals"; a couple of
yellow brick planters ("Built 'em myself—
not bad for an old man, eh?"); fine-grained
walnut paneling; and sliding glass-door cabinets
suspended over the long oak kitchen counter . . .

The master bedroom, once evidently two ("I
knocked down that wall with my own two hands!"),
looks unslept-in . . .
                        In the spare, rumpled den,
an unmade daybed, a closetful of shirts.

A few tiles missing in the shower.

"To tell you the truth, I lost interest when
the Doll died. That's why I'm selling . . . I used to
fix up every little thing—now I don't care.
I could call my son, and move in with him
tonight—he keeps asking. Don't you believe me?
Look, I'm picking up the phone . . ."

                        *

"Twenty-five years—and he's selling the house
right out from under us!
                        All my friends
live on this street; my kids' friends . . .

                        My husband
had a restaurant around the corner, three blocks
from here. It burned down two years ago—
we still haven't collected the insurance;
now he's driving a cab. We'd buy the house
ourselves if we had any money.

Who thinks they'll ever have to move . . .
                        There's so much
stuff! We've still got all the kids' toys.

                   At least
we won't have to pay these heating bills. Winters
it's freezing in here! This year
we were going to close off the living room
on account of the cold.

                  I feel sorry for anyone
moving here!

          It's all his son's idea . . . If
he died, my sister and me would get half
the house; but if he sells it, he could leave
all the money to his son!

               What can you do—
you have to make the best.

               He drinks, did you
notice? A certified alky! Even before my
mother died . . . Believe me, he was never the
greatest husband in the world.

               We get so
worried about him, alone down there . . . He's
fallen a dozen times, and he won't
let us in—thinks we're spying on him.

He just can't be trusted. Changes his mind
every five seconds—
                   you know, at the last minute
he could decide not to sell!

I'll be glad
to see him taken care of, though; I just hope
that son of his knows what kind of a bargain
he's getting . . .

            Listen, is there any chance
you could let us stay? We've been good tenants—
fix things ourselves; always pay the rent on time . . .

Of course, it would depend on how much you were
planning to raise it. We could even squeeze in
downstairs, if you needed *our* place; put in
a daybed until my son leaves home;
                        make do!

We've done it before . . . At least we could stay
in our own neighborhood, our own house.
                              It would be
awful to have to move—awful to move away."

AT THE WINDOW

(from "Crossing the Rockies")

Aurora. Roseville.
"Magic City." Sweetgrass Hills.

"Where's your husband?"
"I haven't got a husband. I never married."

Winter Park ("The Ice-box of America"). Bulk Anti-freeze.
Icicle Canyon.

"John, not now, not before breakfast. I want to shake this cold."

Lovelock. Tunnel City.
Tangent. Helper.

"I hate having people do things for me, cutting my steak . . . I had a stroke—can you tell? Let's not talk about it . . . My late husband and I both came from these parts. Anyone ever tell you how the Grand Tetons got their name? (Maybe I shouldn't!) This Frenchman looked up at the mountains and said, 'What *big tits!*'"

Three Sisters Mountains. Missouri Breaks.
Diamond Peak.

"I wonder, what's the 'regional specialty' for the Donner Pass?"

Whitefish. Soda Springs.
Two Medicine River.

"I crossed the head of that river—and the mouth."

Osceola. Ottumwa.
Winnemucca. Truckee.

"I built that bank . . . the building . . . my firm did."

Floor Systems Repair. Kish & Sons Electric.
Sparks.

"We're the Crook twins, C-R-O-O-K . . . just like the word."

Commerce City. Nugget Casino and Hotel.
Price.

Child (playing *Trivial Pursuits*): "What's the President's official theme song?"
Mother: "'We're in the Money!'"

"Pig Capital of the World." "Smelt Capital of the World."
"Lumber Capital of the U.S." "Egg Capital of the World."
"Apple Capital of the World."

"I'm a Congressman—retired. I could've run again if I wanted to. Too much flying back and forth, though. I don't fly anywhere anymore unless I have to. That's why I voted against the airline appropriation . . ."

Trojan Nuclear Power Plant. Koch Oil Refinery.
"Biggest Little City in the World."

". . . It's the Weimar Republic!"

Geneva. Havre.
Malta. Glasgow.

"We're both retired. Well, I've been retired all my life. We're newlyweds, actually—just celebrating our first anniversary."

Fort Union (new time zone). *Grand Junction.*

"You should go at Mardi Gras."
"That's what everyone tells me—but I get so nervous in crowds."

Izaak Walton Inn. Polish Museum.
Emigrant Gap. Blackfeet Indian Writing Co.

"Come from Alaska. Ketchikan. Goin' to Florida . . . Son's in Florida. Lake Okeechobee . . . Got some time on my hands—do a little fishin'—meet people, talk to people . . ."

The Bar of America. Saint James Hotel.
Frank Pure Food Company (Franksville). ZELDA'S DINER: OPEN.

FOURTEEN PEOPLE

(after a portrait series by Ralph Hamilton)

RALPH HAMILTON

It's all in the eyes. The broad, smudged,
helpless body shivers and dissolves, washing out
its thin, coloring-book outlines; arms hang
stiff at the sides; vest (popped?) open; broad
white tie tight under a shovel of red beard;
feet apart, planted—barely—in Japanese sandals.
(An "aesthetic" touch? or homey, summery—
countering the long-sleeved Windsor formality?)
But the eyes: coal-blue, white-hot, sapphire coals,
shifting behind the flat front of flesh—
untouchable; unshakable . . .
                    The disappearing artist
keeping close behind the flimsy painted cardboard
with holes poked-out only for the eyes.

LLOYD SCHWARTZ

Something behind the philosophical glasses' glass
draws one in; the whole "look" centripetal—
condensing, concentrating, the head a small nebula,
"nebulous" in its rusty cloud of hair and beard.
While the *art nouveau* body—high-necked, courtly—
pretty shaky, really; hardly a leg to stand on,
brushed—as they are—out from under, centrifugally,
into the surrounding swirl; hands hanging on
to each other (fused, practically) for dear life . . .
Outside (wasn't this painted indoors?) it's all gray.
A storm's coming, or going. His lips are trembling.
Cold? But his collar's open, trousers summer-white.
The storm's inside—if there is a storm.
Something in the eyes has nothing to do with weather.

GAIL MAZUR

The knowing eye, barely perceptible under dark shades;
a radiant magenta jacket, loosely knotted over
billowing, shimmery "cerulean" pants; dark hair pouring
over delicate, sexy shoulders. A celebrity? A star?
What's the joke she's almost keeping to herself?
And yet, one hand (girlishly, nervously) clutches a finger
of the other. And, aren't the shoulders slightly "pinched"?
Knees too close? And the smile, uncertain? The dark glasses
forbidding? Her face crossed by too many shadows . . .
She wants to—she wants *us* to—step back, step back
and see her shine (she is shining). She wants
room to shine.

        While that wide eye, that shadowed eye, sees
into the dark, sees a dark her own beams can't reach.

"I look like I've had a spike driven down the back
of my head!" And he accepts it, this picture,
likes it. It's him, though the jaw and lips
have been smeared downward; the brow, the eyes
knotted, unwilling to alter their gaze.
The sloping, bewildered shoulders anticipate—and give
in to—their mysterious, wearying burden.
Collar open; jacket open; hands empty, and open.
He makes his way through a thick fog, through
the canvas—toward us; wearing, like the air itself,
the bleak color of earth. How much sorrow can he stand,
this night-walker, before he can't separate himself
from his sorrow? . . . this ghost, this pale, empty-handed
monster, stumbling forward with his monstrous grief.

JANE STRUSS

> *Now the sun rises, rises so bright,*
> *As if no misfortune had come in the night.*
> *Misfortune has come, come only to me—*
> *But the sun shines for all, for all to see.*

The spotlight is so bright I can hardly see;
but haven't I seen enough already? My mother
an alcoholic, a suicide; my son retarded;
marriage a joke; my Cinderella daughter
farmed out by her next mother to strangers.
Some of this I chose—losing that wasting world
to sing Orpheus; Dido's lament, and Phaedra's—
a woman's love and life; the death of children;

songs of a wayfarer; the song of the Earth.
My suburban Dorabella was a fiasco (I tried
to stab myself with a spoon!). Pathetic at comedy,
with tragedy I'm right at home: serious songs,
the skull under the skin. Look at my eyes—
see what I have seen; see what I see. Listen!

MR. AND MRS. HAMILTON

They're quite a pair. He's the quiet one—
the Scottish side; though the two or three times
he lost his temper, his rage was terrifying.
He's so shaky now . . . Most evenings he'll sit home
watching something—hockey, or baseball—on TV
and won't open his mouth, except for his nightcap.
She'll come charging in, stand in front of the set,
tell him something, sit down with a huge sigh
or groan, doze off (I've mostly painted her asleep),
get up, go out to the kitchen, spread a couple of
thick pats of butter on a piece of white bread
(the French side), come back with a diet soda,
and collapse into a chair with another heaving sigh.
At the end of the movie, she'll wake up
and go to bed upstairs. He'll sleep on the couch.

Neither one was ever particularly affectionate.
He's so bottled up; she so loud, so aggressive.
Once, when I was little, I came up behind where
she was sitting, and threw my arms around her.
She jumped three feet into the air! She thought
I was going to kill her; I had nightmares for weeks.
Now she's retired too, and things at home are even

more difficult. She got me so mad, I had to
put off painting her for a month—I was afraid
I might be unfair. Though this time, I think
I've almost captured her—her energy; her power.
People tell me *he's* my best subject, my most
touching. Ten years ago, his shadow had my profile;
now all our portraits have the same shadow.

JOYCE PESEROFF

"Look at that yellow shirt!" "Banana." "No ... *canary*;
and those vanilla slacks." "Slack? That hard crease
could hold her up." "Neat; perfect posture. But easy,
comfortable—shirt out, short sleeves, earth shoes,
that mushroom-cloud of hair ..." "What about those buttons—
all buttoned; and her arms at attention, one foot forward.
I bet she's itching for a fight ..." "Or ready for one;
I wouldn't mess with those laser slit-eyes." "But where's
her face? It seems ... unfinished; almost un-formed."
"She wants it that way: for surprises." "Or secrets ..."
"Her lips ("Lips? *Where?*" "Don't be funny.") are sealed.
She has to be wary." "*Chary* ... She won't give an inch."
"She can't—she's on an edge. There's nothing behind her."
"Not about to fall though." "No, unassailable." "Scary ..."

ROBERT PINSKY

> *". . . that rarest category of talents, a poet-critic."*

Demonstrating this talent *vis-à-vis* your portrait, as in
       your wicked
"light-eating silence" parody ("composed in less time than
       it takes
to type"), you went straight for the jugular: the "tense
       jaw,"
"iron smile," and "mask-like" face. I'd found it sweeter—
       innocent white
and blue (short sleeves and jeans); round brown eyes averted
       in athletic
humility; a touch, maybe, of the tennis-court conqueror's
       acknowledgment
of adulation; but more Greek bronze (*kouros*) than bronzed
       Berkeley prince.

You've often bent your irony toward yourself. Who else would
       crack jokes
about calling his next book by his first name? Is this pose
       putting on
what enemies take you for: All-American (Jewish) Success?
       Lucky S.O.B.
waiting for the prizes to roll in? Success, friends agree,
       suits you—
though it's been painting you further up the ladder from
       reach.
Your "mask" tells what vigilance against fatigue, distraction,
       discouragement
the competitor maintains, to protect his skill, his sanity, and
       his art.

MARGO LOCKWOOD

"The Melancholy Life-of-the-Party," her familiar rosy flush
muted here, transmogrified into Watteau's hapless, quizzical
Italian Comedian . . . pearl-pale Pierrot, in white Commedia smock.
Black Irish, though, the glint and head-tilt. Black eyebrow
up for all the latest (jokes, poems, gossip); dark, roving eye
out, casting for the day's trouble. Tight-lipped, downcast heroine
of her own Pearl White cliffhanger: WIDOWED MOTHER OF FOUR
AND THE MORTGAGE DUE . . . Breathless, hairbreadth, in-one-door-
out-the-other escape-artist star of that long-running farce,
The Horse in the Attic, her failing Brookline bookshop (also with a
storied past). At the hard-core tail end of a Cambridge party,
belting Cole Porter, lounge-style: "What's the good of swank, or
cash in the bank galore?" GROUCHO, CHICO, HARPO . . . AND MARGO,
bowing out with this week's latest, un-secret word: "Fuckoleum!"

TOM JOANIDES

Which of these statements is true?

(a) I just got off the boat from Albania; (b) I look like
I just got off the boat from Albania; (c) I'm a master potter,
baking porcelains in a kiln I built myself; (d) I'm a master
pastry chef, sampling desserts I bake for a famous
downtown hotel; (e) I live on donuts, sometimes one or two
dozen at a time; (f) I'm a diet freak, starving myself
on tofu and brown rice, purging my system with gallons of warm
salted water; (g) I'm an actor—a good one; (h) I've played an
amazing joke: I came home with someone I'd just met, went
into the bathroom, and shaved off my beard; (i) All my clothes
come from Goodwill; (j) I drive a Mercedes; (k) I'm the
artist's oldest friend; (l) I'm unhappy, I hate my life; (m)
Everything changes—give me a minute; (n) None of this is true.

"ARDIE" MATTEOSIAN

This one's my favorite. It's so loving: the generous pink dress,
silver-white hair, rose-thin lipstick . . . painted with such care.
Those subtle white lines—guidelines?—mapping her face and neck.
("I had to be dragged in to pose; then dragged back to see it.
I didn't want to be painted. I had on a zebra-striped dress
that made me look like an awning; thank God he changed it.")
Her "carriage," the humble way she's got both hands in front of her
holding her glasses. ("So professional! As if I'd been called away
from my desk; which I *was*. Not that I have to work; I'd go crazy
without something to do, something useful, to get me through the day.")
And her eyes, her *eye*—so forthright, and sad; as if she'd seen
something, and can't say what it is, or look away. Her other eye
already obliterated in its shadow. ("I don't know, I don't know
anything. Why would anyone want to paint me? Who'd want to look?")

DANNY AND MARY KELLEHER

Your intimidating teacher—bald; bird-like; bell-bottomed;
double-shirted (no longer the fashion). Crossed arms; piercing,
imperious eyes (some things never change). The lines in his face
glaring white neon . . . *She's* changed. Where's the caustic
blond pixie (his precocious student)? Sketch-pad wild with color—
jungles of animals, sexual landscapes. Later, sparrow skeletons
and dead mice, drawn from life; half-worked poems; elementary
guitar; tarot cards and bird mask (ominous, home-made). Not yet
this waif, waiting by the eternal roadside—a glittering, low-
necked cocktail dress half-hidden under her sagging carcoat.

Remember the late-Sunday-afternoon wine and gossip? The kids into
everything—the encyclopedia; the refrigerator; the conversation.
(Who's knifing Who in the cutthroat art marketplace? Who got
the grant *you* deserved?) The walls generously hung with students
and friends (some already "names"). His own outsize
ethereal abstractions stashed in a hallway—too big to put up,
or give away. Remember what confusion when one actually sold?

When was it they moved to the further suburbs? Decided to adopt
a "troubled teenager"? The nuclear family, detonating:
midnight hospital rushes (the youngest's asthma; an older one's
arm, shredded); stalled cars, and salaries; studios abandoned.

He was your best, your toughest teacher. Her vivid pastels
even you were willing to trade your paintings for.

They wanted to be artists, and people. We used to visit them . . .

Now they're frescoes. Earthy, luminescent greens and browns,
pale pre-Renaissance skin, fleshed from the muddy plaster;
unhappy, fallen Adam and Eve; a disapproving Angel delivering
merciless Annunciations to his sullen, empty-eyed Madonna.

GOODNIGHT, GRACIE

for Gracie Allen (1906–1964)

"Almost everything I know today I learned by listening
to myself when I was talking about things I didn't under-
stand."

"Mrs. Burns, I love that zany character of yours."
"So do I, or else I wouldn't have married him."

"You mean you understand it?"
"Well, of course! When I misunderstand what you say, I al-
ways know what you're talking about."

Home very late from a Hollywood party, George and Gracie
can hear their phone ringing, but can't find the key
to get in. George is vexed, and tired, but Gracie is dying
to wake Blanche Morton next door and gossip about dancing
with Gary Cooper: "His belt buckle ruined my gardenia!"
Soon the Mortons are locked out ("Gracie, did you close
the door?" "No, but I will!"); the locksmith's tools locked in
(will his jealous new wife ever believe this?); and the
phone never stops . . . Day breaks, and George breaks in
through a window. "I've got a wonderful idea," he announces.
"From now on, we'll leave a door-key under the mat." "But I
put one there *months* ago," Gracie argues, "and we couldn't
get in last night." The telephone again: who's been trying
to get through? "Gracie, who was on the phone?" "*I* was."

*

"It's not a matter of whether I'm right or wrong—it's a matter of principle."

"Men are so deceitful. They look you right in the eye while they're doing things behind your back."

"Don't rush me. It isn't easy to make up the truth."

Ronnie's dying for a part in a new play whose famous author
is fascinated by Gracie; but the only role still open is intended
for a middle-aged actress, sole support of her widowed mother . . .
"I'm a widow too," Gracie fibs, "and Ronnie supports me!" Smitten,
the playwright invites her to dine in his room. "My husband died
in a shipwreck," she embroiders, "on our honeymoon." "Lucky
you survived!" "Oh, I wasn't there." In breezes Ronnie,
and asks for "Dad." Gracie (thinking fast): "He can never forget
his father." Playwright (bewildered): "But he never knew him."
Gracie (triumphant): "If he knew him, he'd forget him!" Enter
"the Widow Morton" with Ronnie's long-lost father, to unravel
Gracie's tangled web . . . Blushing, the playwright offers Ronnie a part;
Ronnie's in heaven; Gracie's forgiven; the playwright, like George
himself, resigned to applaud her irresistible assassinations.

*

"I may not be here long."
"Where are you going?"
"Oh, don't I wish I knew!"

"I didn't think people felt this wonderful when they were going. But, then again, this is the first time I've gone."

"If you ask me a question and I don't answer, don't be nervous. Just take your hats off."

... how casually we treated Gracie's illness. Those pills made me feel very secure. I figured we could go on this way year after year—it never entered my mind that anything would change it. Then one evening Gracie had another one of her attacks. I gave her the pill, we held on to each other—but this time it didn't work. When the pain continued, I called Dr. Kennamer, and they rushed Gracie to the hospital. . . . Two hours later Gracie was gone.

"He's crazy about dancing. His new wife has got to be a
very good dancer." Gracie thinks she's dying—having opened
by mistake Harry von Zell's telegram meant to save George
from a weekend seasick on his sponsor's yacht: EXAMINED YOUR
WIFE CONDITION SERIOUS URGE YOU DO NOT LEAVE HER . . . "I'm a
very sick woman, but my health is so good, I didn't even know it!"
She's had three agencies send over their most attractive
candidates to replace "the late Mrs. Burns": "Sounds like it
won't be easy to fill *her* shoes." "What size do you wear?"
"How old was she when she passed on?" "Well, I'd rather not say—
she hasn't passed on far enough for that." George, however,
has already chosen his next wife, who—relieved, reprieved—
would rather George hadn't explained: "It's such a letdown. After
this, how can I be gay about an ordinary thing like living?"

LOVE

"Why live? I never really thought.
I never went to church, or read books.
I worked, for a railroad; but work
was like sleepwalking.
I took drugs and drove around.
I married a girl who loved me.
Why? I wasn't very good to her
most of the time. And she died."

"I wasn't very pretty, or 'bright.'
School meant nothing, I couldn't wait
till it was over. After graduation,
I went to work for my father.
I needed to get out.
I can remember a fight about a car;
I wanted one so badly, and they knew
it was so I could be with him."

"Sometimes I felt grateful—even if she
was a little overweight;
I wasn't such a winner myself.
We broke up a couple of times. I
hit her once, when we were stoned . . .
After we got married, I had myself dried out.
We got more serious. We were even
planning to get married again in church."

"Things got better after he got
off the drugs. Things also
didn't change. Friday night: bowling, or a
hockey game. Saturday: a movie, double date.
Sunday: my parents, who were beginning
to 'accept the situation.'
Nothing happened; only sometimes
it happened more peacefully."

"What could I do? She was already dead
in the ambulance. Never sick a day
in her life! Who could believe this?
I knew they'd blame me. No one said a word;
but I knew.
Everyone said it was terrible—
but that I was young; I should be patient;
I'd get over it."

"I felt dizzy . . . We were in the kitchen,
talking, while I was making dinner
(I was a terrible cook).
I said I was feeling dizzy. It was getting
harder to breathe. I remember falling,
and him leaning over me, saying my name,
asking what's the matter? I remember thinking
someone should turn off the stove."

"I put my flower on her casket,
like everyone else. Even the priest
was upset. She was so young!
He asked me to come and see him . . .
Nobody could know what we felt.
I don't think I knew myself.
All I could think was
I wanted to be with her—inside."

"Why did you do it?"
"I had to be with you."

"You were so young."
"I couldn't wait."

"You were alive . . ."
"The world was a coffin."

"Did it hurt much?"
"I don't remember, now."

PSEUDODOXIA EPIDEMICA

It is evident not only in the general frame of Nature, that things most manifest unto sense have proved obscure unto the understanding.
—Sir Thomas Browne

"Hi."
"Hi."

"You OK?"
"I guess . . . You?"

"I miss you."
"I miss you too."

"What are you doing?"
"Reading . . . You?"

"*The Late Show*."
". . . What time will you be home?"

"Around dinner. Eat out?"
"I guess."

"The movie's starting."
"Thanks for calling."

"See you tomorrow."
"See you."

*

Sorry I won't be here when you
get home. I need time to think. Please
don't try to reach me—I'll keep calling
till I reach you, to explain.
        Don't worry!

                Love

*The common opinion of the Oestridge, or Sparrow-Camel,
conceives that it digesteth Iron; and this is confirmed by the
affirmations of many; beside swarms of others.*

"Hi,
it's me . . ."

"Where are you?"
"I'd rather not say."

"Why aren't you here?"
"I'll tell you when I see you."

"When?"
"Whenever you want."

"Now."

". . . Are you angry?"
"I'll tell you when I see you."

Moles are blind, and have no eyes.

"—How could you
do this to me?"

"Do you want me to come back?"

"I'm so angry, I could
kill you!"

"Do you want me to come back?"

"No! Yes.
—How could you do this to me?"

"Do you want me to come back?"

> Concerning the Chameleon, there generally passeth an
> opinion that it liveth only upon air.

"I'm sorry . . . Do you
believe me? I'm really sorry—
I didn't want to hurt you; I just
didn't care."

". . . But why do you want to see me?"

"Sometimes, I just like
to be with you."

"I like to be with you too."

". . . You do?"
"Yes."

In every place we meet with the picture of the Pelican,
opening her breast with her bill and feeding her young
ones with the blood distilling from her.

    L—dear
        I tried to find
  the list with Michael's
     number on it to call you
        because I was worried—
           Please have pity on me
             I do a lot of really wrong things
               —but have very little
                  pity on myself
                    C

A Loadstone, held in the hand, doth either cure or give
great ease in the Gout, or as an amulet it also cureth the
head-ache; for perceiving its secret power to draw magneti-
cal bodies, men have invented a new attraction, to draw
out the dolour and pain of any part.
                   And therefore upon
this stone they graved the Image of Venus.

The further away you get, the more I need you:

the further away I get you, the more you need.
The further away I need you, the more you get:

the further away you need, the more I get you.

The more I get you, the further away you need:

the more you get, the further away I need you.
The more you need, the further away I get you:

the more I need you, the further away you get.

SIMPLE QUESTIONS

Can you hear me? Do you
understand?

How are you feeling? Can you
feel anything?

Are you in pain? Is there anything
I can do?

Do you know me? Do you
know who I am?

*

When I dream about my father, he's
recovered. Home. He can move—walk; talk to
my mother; complain; even argue.
(The doctor at the hospital, not encouraging,
wouldn't deny this possibility.)

He comes downstairs and makes his way
toward his favorite chair, the one
with the florid cushions he'd stitched himself.
His breath comes hard, as it had
in the hospital; but suddenly, miraculously—

better!

I started having this dream
after my first visit.

*

"What comes after seven? Say it.
Try! What's the number after seven? . . . That's

right! Now what comes after eight? Tell me,
what comes after eight? . . ."

Once my mother got him to count
to fifteen.

Then, seven.

*

He was the old man you'd pass as you
hurried down the corridor to see your friend
in traction (touch football
terpsichore), or with pneumonia (not, thank God,
critical); the old man with the sucked-in
yellow face, no teeth, the oxygen tube
up his nose, the urine sac hanging from his bed.
Breathing hard; hardly moving; his eyes
blank, yet (weren't they?) following you . . .

Not your own.

The unhappy family whose
trouble he was . . .

NOT YOUR OWN.

*

"Hello! Say hello. How do you
feel? Are you feeling better?"

"A little better."

"Good." She leans over and
looks into his face. "Did you sleep OK?"

No answer.

"Do you know me? Who
am I? What's my name?"

"M-mom."

"And what's your name? Can you
tell me your name?"

"Sam."

"Good! Are you hungry? Let me give you
some soup? A little custard? . . ."

"No."

"Are you thirsty? Where's your straw?
Would you like some juice?"

"Yes."

"How about a nice shave? Would you
like me to give you a shave? . . . There!

Now you look handsome!"

He rubs his face with his right hand;
he keeps rubbing his face.

                    *

"Are you the son? What a pity! He seems like
such a nice person, such a sweet old man.
It's a shame . . . Last night he was very quiet—
slept like a baby. Didn't bother anybody!
By the end of the week he'll be ready to go home."

                    *

"Wake up! Open your eyes. Can you
keep your eyes open?"

No answer.

"Look at me. Can you see me? Who
am I? Do you know who I am?"

No answer.

"Can you hear me? Do you understand
what I'm saying to you?"

". . . Yes."

"Look around. Where are you?
Do you know where you are?"

No answer.

"Can you feel anything? Can you feel
my hand? Where's my hand?"

I put my hand in his; he
squeezes hard.

"Who am I? Do you know who I am?"

". . . Yes."

"What's my name? Say it. Who
am I? Tell me who I am."

". . . Fa-ther."

*

No love lost. A lifetime of
anger; resentment; disapproval. Could I pretend—
even now—a deep, personal concern?

Prodding him to speech (what the doctor
ordered), to recover enough of his mind to
help my mother endure his release,

hypnotized me, gripped my attention, the way
his right hand gripped my hand—the last remnant
of his unrelenting, fist-clenched

denunciations of the world:

of the "Hitler Brothers," who refused him even
a moment's rest in the sweatshops where he
spent his working life stitching men's clothes;

of relatives, or neighbors, never generous or
grateful enough, for someone rarely generous
or grateful; of my friends, of *me*—stymied by my

anger; resentment; disapproval . . . The way
his right hand gripped the hedgecutter, lifted it,
and aimed it at my head.

"I have to go now. Goodbye! I'll see you
tomorrow . . . Do you hear me?
Feel better. I hope you feel better."

       *

"How do you feel? Talk to me. Tell me
how you feel."

". . . Not so good."

"Are you in pain? Where does
it hurt you?"

No answer.

"Can I do anything? Should I
get the doctor?"

". . . No doctor can cure me."

       *

"He had a restless night; couldn't swallow—
we had to pump out his throat. His pressure
sank way down. There was nothing else we
could do . . . I'm sorry. He just fell
asleep, very peaceful, and stopped breathing."

*

"Can you hear me?"
"Yes."

"How are you feeling?"
"A little better."

"Do you know me? Who am I?"
"My son."

"Is there anything I can do?"
"No."

from Cairo Traffic (2000)

for Ralph Hamilton

A TRUE POEM

I'm working on a poem that's so true, I can't show it to anyone.

I could never show it to anyone.

Because it says exactly what I think, and what I think scares me.

Sometimes it pleases me.

Usually it brings misery.

And this poem says exactly what I think.

What I think of myself, what I think of my friends, what I think about my lover.

Exactly.

Parts of it might please them, some of it might scare them.

Some of it might bring misery.

And I don't want to hurt them, I don't want to hurt them.

I don't want to hurt anybody.

I want everyone to love me.

Still, I keep working on it.

Why?

Why do I keep working on it?

Nobody will ever see it.

Nobody will ever see it.

I keep working on it even though I can never show it to anybody.

I keep working on it even though someone might get hurt.

FRIENDLY SONG ("CANÇAO AMIGA")*

by Carlos Drummond de Andrade

I'm working on a song
in which my own mother sees her image,
everyone's mother sees her image,
and it speaks, it speaks just like two eyes.

I'm traveling along a roadway
that winds through many countries.
My old friends—if they don't see me,
I see them, I see and salute them.

I am giving away a secret
like someone who loves, or smiles.
In the most natural way
two caresses reach each other.

My whole life, all of our lives
make up a single diamond.
I've learned a few new phrases—
and to make others better.

I'm working on a song
that wakes men up
and lets children sleep.

* printed on the Brazilian 50 Cruzados note.

SHE FORGETS

The one who told me about the Holocaust, who taught me moral distinctions, who gave me music and told me jokes, is in a nursing home: lonely, scared, surrounded only by people so much worse off (inarticulate, incapacitated, drooling), she thinks she's in a crazy house.

She's not crazy.

She's there—I put her there—because she can't take care of herself, can't be left alone.

She's old.

She forgets.

She forgets her medicine.

She forgets what she's not supposed to eat.

She forgets what day it is.

She remembers who she is—and who she was—and knows she's not herself.

She can't remember what's wrong with her ("What's wrong with me, honey?") or why she's there, but she knows her brain isn't working right.

Her brain needs air.

Oxygen has a hard time squeezing through her hardened arteries.

So her blood congeals.

Little clots cause little strokes, which destroy her memory.

Aspirin, which thins the blood and helps keep the oxygen flowing, might help her remember.

But she's old.

Part of her stomach has turned upside down.

Her food gets stuck in her chest, blocks her breath.

She panics, forces herself to vomit, which makes her bleed—which damages her heart.

A simple operation could fix her stomach.

But doctors won't operate on someone with a damaged heart.

And aspirin makes her bleed.

So she can't take aspirin.

So she forgets.

I live in another city.

Once, after I came to visit, she wasn't thinking about her food.

She ate too much, or too fast, and the food wouldn't go down.

So she panicked, forced herself to vomit, and had a heart attack.

She was in the hospital for three weeks (which she doesn't remember).

So I've had to put the one who gave me music and told me jokes, who taught me moral distinctions, and warned me never to forget the Holocaust—I've had to put her in a nursing home, a crazy house, where she's scared and lonely; where she stares out the window and asks: "*What day is today?*"

"*Why can't I go home?*"

"*What's wrong with me, honey?*"

"*Why am I here?*"

THE TWO HORSES (A MEMORY)

You said you had lunch in Pittsfield, was it on North Street?

That reminds me of when we lived on the farm.

It must be eighty years ago.

We went to a one-room schoolhouse, didn't you drive past it once?

Each row was a different grade.

I sat in the first seat of the first row.

The teacher's name was Miss Brown.

She was so pretty.

I wonder if she's still alive.

The day before we left the farm our cat disappeared.

We couldn't find her anywhere.

I was sad for weeks.

Three months later she showed up at our new house in Pittsfield.

Robbins Avenue.

I can't think of the number now.

My sister was in New York.

She didn't like the people she was living with so she'd visit us.

She fell in love with the young man who lived next door.

Maurice.

Your uncle Maurice.

They got married and moved to Cleveland.

They're both gone now, aren't they?

You know, I can't picture her.

A few years later we moved to New York.

This just jumped into my mind: I must have been three years old.

We were still in Russia.

Mir.

A small town, but famous for its yeshiva.

My oldest brother—Joe—took our horses down to the river.

They were the two best horses in the town.

My father had a phaeton.

A beautiful old buggy.

He was like a taxi driver, he took people to Minsk.

Or Vilna.

That day he was at the station.

The passenger station, waiting for customers.

My brother was still just a kid.

He must have been washing the horses in the river.

I can remember—it was a hot day.

Maybe he was giving them a drink.

And while I was watching the reins got caught around a pole in the river.

The horses kept twisting the reins around that pole.

It was slippery, the reins kept sliding down under the water and they were pulling the horses down with them.

I ran into town and got my father who came running back with a knife in his teeth.

He jumped into the river with all his clothes on.

He took the knife and sawed away at the reins until he finally cut through.

He saved the horses.

I haven't thought about this in a thousand years.

It's like a dream: you get up it's forgotten.

Then it all comes back.

Didn't I ever tell you?

Look at me, I'm starting to cry.

What's there to cry about?

Such an old, old memory, why should it make me cry?

HE TELLS HIS MOTHER WHAT HE'S WORKING ON

I'm writing a poem about you.

You are? What's it about?

It's the story about your childhood, the horses in the river.

The ones that nearly drowned? . . . I saved them.

You told it to me just a few weeks ago.

I should dig up more of my memories.

I wish you would.

Like when I lived on the farm and one of the girls fell down the well?

Yes.

I forget if it was Rose or Pauline—it was a deep well.

I remember that story.

Have you finished your poem?

I'm still working on it.

You mean you're correcting it, with commas and semi-colons?

Exactly.

When can I see it?

As soon as it's finished.

Is it an epic?

It's not that long.

No, I mean all my thoughts, the flashes of what's going through my life, the whole family history . . . living through the woe, the river and the water.

I know.

Will it be published?

I have to finish it first.

It's better to write about real life, that's more important than writing something fanciful.

I try to write all my poems about real life.

You see, the apple never falls far from the tree.

I guess not.

You're my apple.

There's probably a worm crawling through that apple.

Then it's got something sweet to chew on.

Well, you're my tree.

Yes, I'm your tree—you're an apple, I'm a tree.

THE TWO CHURCHES (A DREAM)

"In the main square, there are two churches, not just one—two
      great Baroque churches, facing each other—decaying,
      yet magnificent. Almost identical, except that one
      is locked, and the door to the other is wide open.

      Early morning, not a cloud in the sky. I'm waiting outside.

      In the center of the square there's a monument,
      an obelisk. Like the 'hand' on a sundial, it casts a

      long, narrow shadow.

It's already quite warm. I look in through the open door,
      peer in: it seems cool and dark inside. But I
      step back, as if I were waiting for someone to arrive.

      But that's impossible—I don't know anyone
      in this town. I can't even speak the language.

A man appears in the doorway—a round,
      ugly little man, with a face like a rubber ball.
      His hair is thin and greasy, his clothes disheveled.

      He has on a white shirt, but it's not tucked in,
      and not recently laundered.
                         His paunch
      hangs over his belt. He wears his pants low,
      to make room for his sagging stomach.

He signals me to come inside.

I don't move. I seem to be staring into the sun.

He comes outside—smiles at me. He's missing
     several front teeth.
               Fat, ugly, dirty—
     yet there's a sweetness, something almost
     cherubic about him. He touches me.
                     He touches
     my shoulder and points inside. Then he nudges me, nudges

     my shoulder, and ushers me into the church.

It isn't dark at all. The light comes
     pouring in. There's no one else inside.

     He guides me around the rim of the nave. Each chapel
     is like a wedding cake, with a
     martyred saint in ecstasy on the top.

With his chubby fingers, he points out
     little details: the pockmark on one saint's face,
     a drop of blood on a bony hand, a crooked
     finger, a fingernail.
                  I'm struck by the
     shafts of light coming in through unseen openings.

     Each time he points, he touches me—nudges me
     with the back of his hand, taps my shoulder, my
     arm, my hip.

He leads me up to the foot of the altar: the body of Jesus
        lying in an open sepulcher.
                        The little man
        stands in front of me, looking into the sepulcher;
        he swings his arm back, and the back of his hand

        accidentally brushes across the front of my pants . . .

He turns and grins. Is he grinning
        at me, or am I just imagining?

He leads me into a side chapel. The window is open,
        but barred. On top of the wedding cake is the Blessed
        Virgin. The little round man stands beside me.

        He points to the Virgin, then swings back his arm until
        the back of his hand touches my chest, presses my chest,

        then slides down, below my waist, and brushes
        across the front of my pants, presses
        against the front of my pants.

        There's no mistake: he's grinning at me, and his
        gap-toothed grin

        is a smile of sexual longing.

I don't move. I don't move
        away. I let him press the back of his hand
        against my pants—against what is growing in my pants.

Suddenly, he drops down on his knees and elbows, like a fat
        puppy—his elbows on the wooden floor,
        his fat rump sticking up into the air. He jiggles his pelvis
        up and down. He turns his head to look

        up at me. He's still grinning, his eyes
        are moist and glistening . . .

        I come around behind him. I bend over him,
        against him, against his fat behind. I wrap my arms
        around his round stomach.

Then we stand up. He unzips his pants and reaches his hand
        inside. I unzip my pants and reach my hand inside.

        He grins. He takes his hand out, looks
        up at the Virgin, and shakes his finger at me:

        'No, no. Not in church.' He grins from ear to

        pudgy ear. He's like one of the mischievous,
        plump-cheeked cherubs over the altar,
        blowing into a trumpet.

I come to him, put my arms around him, *embrace* him. He
        puts his arms around me—his mouth is wet; his lips
        are wet; his tongue is thick and wet.

        There's no one in the church.

        The light is pouring in.

He pushes me by the shoulder into the next chapel: St. Francis—
        with moist red lips, flushed, looking down at us

with large, sad, yearning eyes:
                              Carved,
the little man tells me, by the great saint-maker
of that town—a cripple, who carved his statues
with his knife strapped to his wrist . . .

I understand every word—although the language is
still obscure.

I can't answer, I only nod.

His eyes light up. He takes my hand and leads me
        down a dark corridor, a bare hallway.

        He rests his hand on my shoulder.
        I rest my hand on his shoulder.

        He rubs my back—slowly,
        up and down. I rub his back.

        He turns and reaches his stubby arms around my neck,
        reaches up and kisses me again,

        before he ushers me out of the church, into
        the daylight, into the warm sunlit square outside.

In the square, there are two churches, not just one—two
        great Baroque churches, facing each other—decaying,
        yet magnificent. Almost identical, except that one

        is locked, and the door to the other is wide open."

PORNOGRAPHY

I. FIRST COUPLE

On his knees, his back to us: the pale honeydew melons of his
        bare buttocks, the shapely, muscular hemispheres—

      the voluptuous center.

His knees push into the worn plush of a velvet cushion
        on the floral Oriental beside her cot.

He twists sideways—*contrapposto*—and bends to put his face
        into her crotch, between her limp legs,

      one hoisted by his right shoulder, the other—more
      like an arm—reaching around his back, her ankle
      resting on his naked hip.

      She's wearing shiny slippers with bows; he has on
      bedroom slippers and socks.

He's got a classic profile: straight nose, sharp chin.
        Cowlick. His hair tapers high on his neck,
        outlines his ear, in the current fashion;
                                 her
        curly bob gives away the date (barely '20s).

His mouth grazes her private hair; lips apart, he
        keeps his tongue to himself.

He's serious: if he were wearing clothes, and she were something
        with pipes, he'd be a plumber's assistant—inspecting,
        studious, intent;
                        nothing erotic in his look, hardly
        aroused at all (a little hard to tell, of course,
        from behind).

Flat on her back, on the dark, fringed spread, gravity
        flattening her breasts, she looks

        uncomfortable, but not unhappy. Her eyes
        check out the camera. Her lips are sealed, yet—

        isn't there?—a trace of smile
        playing around the edges . . .

She stretches out an arm to him, places her palm
        flat on his head—guiding him so lightly, she

        might be blessing him.

II. SECOND COUPLE: THE SAILOR AND HIS GIRL

They're hot, half-dressed (upper half only), and they
        can't wait.

        He sports a sailor's midi and a mariner's
        beret (is that a mound of fishing nets
        she's lying back on?)
                        He rests his naked knee
        beside her ample thigh.

Her dress is long—Victorian and striped. If she hadn't
        raised it to her chest, it would be hiding her
        black knee-length stockings and black, mannish shoes.
        (He's also wearing shoes. How did he get his
        pants off?)
                        No underwear—
                                        nothing fallen around her ankles
        to keep her from spreading her legs.

Not quite supine, she strains forward to eye, and
        hold, his bold erection:
                                        bat and hardballs—
        major league (his Fenway Frank; his juicy
        all-day-sucker).

He looks down hungrily at her hungry eyes
        and mouth—one hand pressed flush against
        his own naked thigh.
                                He slouches a little (not all of him is
        standing at attention), to make what she wants
        easier for her to reach.

But the photographer is sharp—he keeps his sharpest focus
        on what he's sure we want it on: all the

        fleshy folds, clefts, crevices—the no-longer-
        secret places—of her welcoming flesh.

He knows the costumes negate the spiritual burden
        (and freedom) of pure nakedness—
                                        put us *in*
        medias res (things happening, things about
        to happen); in

on the guilty secret, complicit—one eye
    furtively glancing over a shoulder . . .

His models rivet their attention on each other (did he
    have to tell them?), so that we can be

    riveted too.

Of course, they're only posing—
    but despite the props and costumes, certain

        undeniable details
        suggest that it isn't—it

    can't be—all an act.

III. MÉNAGE À TROIS

It's the heavy one—the one with the little pot belly, sagging
    breasts, and double chin (practically all we can
    see of her face)—that he's kissing so passionately.

Yet his arms are around them both, he loves them both
    (and of course he couldn't kiss them
    both at the same time).

Naked except for (like them) shoes and stockings, and garters,
    he sits at the edge of an overstuffed easy chair,
    his knees spread wide,
                    his massive cock
    rising like the Leaning Tower from his gut.

His chest and neck, calves and thighs, have an athlete's
sculptured musculature:

exercise keeps all his parts in shape.

Both women are on their knees. She—the heavy one on his
        left (*our* right)—pushes into him, her round belly
        against his knee, her plush, round bottom
        a luxurious counterweight.

        Her fingers clutch his engorged organ, hang
        on to it, almost to steady herself.

The other one is slimmer, prettier, she has a pretty
        mouth—a delicate movie-star face.

        She's almost crouching, practically sitting on her
        own high heels; her right hand tenderly envelopes
        his testicles.
                        Hard to tell if she's smiling
        up at his face or down at his genitals—probably
        both, in equal admiration, adoration, desire.

His own benign, blissed-out look is
        harder to read, his shadowy profile
        half-buried in the intense kiss.

There's something sweet, *humane*, about them all: not
        innocent—
                        but nothing (well, almost nothing) hard,
        or hardened yet.

Only the little they have on reminds us how
openly this was intended to be obscene.

The composition itself is elegant—balanced, symmetrical:
    the sweeping curve of the pretty one's behind
    and back, flowing up and across the curve of the
    man's shoulders and neck,
                        then down again through the
    fuller arcs of the plump one's back and rump—

    a harmonious circle of arms: theirs behind his back
    supporting him; his around them—his hands resting
    on their shoulders; their hands meeting in his lap . . .

It's like some medieval *Descent from the Cross* or *Holy*
    Burial: the slumping Christ between two
    ministering Angels—
                  but inside out, inverted, a negative
    of the Passion. Passion here only—and nothing
    but—passion. Perhaps

    not even passion.

This ancient postcard: cracked; corners broken; edges
    frayed; worn and fragile

    from use.

    How many has it gratified; disappointed;
    hurt? In whose horny fingers has it

    been gripped (and did that hand
    know what the other was doing)?

Not innocent—

      but nothing about them
      hard, or hardened yet;

      not yet past taking pleasure
      in whatever pleasure they

      receive, or give.

PROVERBS FROM PURGATORY

It was déjà vu all over again.

I know this town like the back of my head.

People who live in glass houses are worth two in the bush.

One hand scratches the other.

A friend in need is worth two in the bush.

A bird in the hand makes waste.

Life isn't all it's crapped up to be.

It's like finding a needle in the eye of the beholder.

It's like killing one bird with two stones.

My motto in life has always been: *Get It Over With*.

Two heads are better than none.

A rolling stone deserves another.

All things wait for those who come.

A friend in need deserves another.

I'd trust him as long as I could throw him.

He smokes like a fish.

He's just a chip off the old tooth.

I'll have him eating out of my lap.

A friend in need opens a can of worms.

Too many cooks spoil the child.

An ill wind keeps the doctor away.

The wolf at the door keeps the doctor away.

People who live in glass houses keep the doctor away.

A friend in need shouldn't throw stones.

A friend in need washes the other.

A friend in need keeps the doctor away.

A stitch in time is only skin deep.

A verbal agreement isn't worth the paper it's written on.

A cat may look like a king.

Know which side of the bed your butter is on.

Nothing is cut and dried in stone.

You can eat more flies with honey than with vinegar.

Don't let the cat out of the barn.

Let's burn that bridge when we get to it.

When you come to a fork in the road, take it.

Don't cross your chickens before they hatch.

DO NOT READ THIS SIGN.

Throw discretion to the wolves.

After the twig is bent, the barn door is locked.

After the barn door is locked, you can come in out of the rain.

A friend in need locks the barn door.

There's no fool like a friend in need.

We've passed a lot of water since then.

At least we got home in two pieces.

All's well that ends.

It ain't over till it's over.

There's always one step further down you can go.

It's a milestone hanging around my neck.

Include me out.

It was déjà vu all over again.

THE DREAM DURING MY MOTHER'S RECUPERATION

At 89, my mother is in the hospital, mysteriously losing blood, when suddenly her stomach hemorrhages. She's rushed into surgery but is not expected to survive. Two years earlier, the hospital cardiologist prevented the operation that might have prevented this emergency: he thought her heart couldn't take it. After the operation, she remains in intensive care for three weeks, most of that time with a breathing tube down her throat so that she can't speak at all, though she can write short, very shaky notes:

TAKE IT OUT   thirsty   put my teeth in my mouth

I'll be here alone

Slowly, to everyone's astonishment, her strength begins to return.

These are some of the things she said to me in the hospital and, later, in the convalescent home:

"Worried about me?"

"It's a tough apple to chew on."

"I'm not doing anything, but I'm doing it the hard way."

"I might as well make a good job as none at all."

"I'm a human being. WORRY is one of my stations."

"I'm a specimen of deliberation."

"I'll sleep my years away."

"I'll let things go the way they come."

"I feel lost. I'm heading for nowhere. I have to stop somewhere to see where I'm landing."

"Whatever is going on will be going on without me."

"It passes so fast. That's life."

"The winter sun is like a stepmother's love."

"I'm one day closer to the end."

"Nothing goes easy for me."

"I can't stuff myself like a turkey."

"Sometimes I wake up and I don't know where I am. Then my mind begins to unravel, and I know where I am. Then there's some distraction, and my thoughts go behind bars."

"I'm not very happy here: people are so snobby, some of them think themselves more than they are. However, I don't give a hoot."

"I don't know what I'm doing. I'm on this side of the wall; I'm on the other side of the wall. I don't know what they want from me."

"I know the feeling, it's staring me in the face. I just can't throw it away."

"Did I just say something stupid?"

"The Cherinskys have been bubbling up in my mind."

"It's good to talk to you, you're giving me a line to live on."

"I'm OK. I'm not a world's winner, but I'm doing OK."

"Well, your mother came back."

"I'm whole again."

"I'm glad I'm not a question mark. I'm a human being."

"A lot of it was you pulling me back into a land of freedom, goodness, and love."

During the later stages of her recuperation, I dream we're about to embark on a long ocean voyage. The moment we board the ship, we're ordered to put on life jackets, or we will not be permitted to continue. Only my mother doesn't have one. I look everywhere. I comb every inch of the ship. I can't find one for her.

"I have so much to look forward to. I'm renewing my life all over again."

"What you hear from me, this is me."

"Let's live and tell these little stories."

NO ORPHEUS

When he sang of what had passed, the trees would lean toward him,
he could suspend the suffering of the damned, he could bring back
the dead.

Don't look back! . . .

Hell is a spotless room
overlooking the ocean; she

wants out.

"I'm heading for nowhere, what do I have
to look forward to?"

She used to have
a future—

and a past. "I'm lost, I'm like
a stranger to myself."

"I'm an
unstationary pedestal."

"My marbles are slowly rolling away."

She's thrown out family
photos; no longer recalls

her husband, or her
maiden name. Still, she wants him

to lead her back.

"When am I going to see you?
Are we a long distance apart from one another?"

He wants her back.

He wants her back . . .

If it took only
not looking back

to lead her back, it would be easy
not to look, not to look

back; but if helping her look
back is the one way he knows to

help her back, then he has to help her
look back.

Where else could she look?

"I'll try not to remember
too many things. I'll just remember

what I can . . ."

Do we—don't we—have more
(he wishes he knew)

than what we can look back to?

HER WALTZ

"This is my dream. I'm dancing!
(Do you know how to dance? Do you
like to dance?) *Waltzing*—
it's like electricity.

It hurts when I walk. So I pick up a chair,
and I start to waltz.
I look in the mirror and there I am,
dancing with a chair!

I say to the mirror: 'I'm not so old.'
But the mirror says: 'Yes you are.
You're old. You're nearly
ninety years old. What are you doing

waltzing around with a chair?'
Now isn't that silly? An old lady.
This is my dream: I see myself in the mirror
waltzing with a chair.

And that's the end of my dream.
I once knew how to dance. I
once knew how to waltz.
And now I shall bid you goodnight."

NOSTALGIA (THE LAKE AT NIGHT)

The black water.

Lights dotting the entire perimeter.

Their shaky reflections.

The dark tree line.

The plap-plapping of water around the pier.

Creaking boats.

The creaking pier.

Voices in conversation, in discussion—two men, adults—serious inflections (the words themselves just out of reach).

A rusty screen-door spring, then the door swinging shut.

Footsteps on a porch, the scrape of a wooden chair.

Footsteps shuffling through sand, animated youthful voices (*how many?*)—distinct, disappearing.

A sudden guffaw; some giggles; a woman's—no, a young girl's—sarcastic reply; someone's assertion; a high-pitched male cackle.

Somewhere else a child laughing.

Bug-zappers.

Tires whirring along a pavement . . . not stopping . . . receding.

Shadows from passing headlights.

A cat's eyes caught in a headlight.

No moon.

Connect-the-dot constellations filling the black sky—the ladle of the Big Dipper not quite directly overhead.

The radio tower across the lake, signaling.

Muffled quacking near the shore; a frog belching; crickets, cicadas, katydids, etc.—their relentless sexual messages.

A sudden gust of wind.

Branches brushing against each other—pine, beech.

A fiberglass hull tapping against the dock.

A sudden chill.

The smell of smoke, woodstove fires.

A light going out.

A dog barking; then more barking from another part of the lake.

A burst of quiet laughter.

Someone in the distance calling someone too loud.

Steps on a creaking porch.

A screen-door spring, the door banging shut.

Another light going out (you must have just undressed for bed).

My bare feet on the splintery pier turning away from the water.

SONG

rain on the lake
room at the lodge
alone in a room
in the lazy light

loons on the lake
geese in the air
moose in the woods
aware   awake

a cry dislodged
from the musty woods
the gamy musk
of the one aroused

the roaming moose
the rooms lit up
the woods awake
in the loony light

the moon dislodged
the lake aflame
the Muse amazed
amused   aroused

RENATO'S DREAM
Brazil, 1991

Such a sweet dream. I dreamed
I was having a conversation
with the great poets—Manuel
Bandeira and Carlos Drummond
de Andrade. "I was born
tired, hungry, and cold," I said.
And Drummond answered, "I too."

TEMPLE OF DENDUR, METROPOLITAN MUSEUM OF ART
(from "Cairo Traffic")

In that giant temperature-controlled greenhouse on the edge of Central Park, such a tiny temple—prettier here than it ever was along the Nile? A gift to us in return for our contribution to the rescue of a greater temple from the flood created by "what must increasingly be regarded as an ecological, sociological, and economic disaster: the Aswan High Dam." I'd always loved it.

So barely back a minute, I go back to the Met, to this mini-temple, with its shallow artificial moat, photos on the wall of its original site and how it was saved, people milling, a guard standing by to make sure no one gets or tries to get inside—so that it won't lose a millimeter, a milligram of dust. Our passion to preserve is practically a religion. We want the Temple of Dendur to last forever. And who am I, materialist that I am, to object?

For the first time, everything in the Egyptian wing makes sense—the statues, the mummy-cloths, even the maps now have a context.

But something else has happened.

No, I haven't converted, though in fact I find I have a lot of sympathy with elements of what I understand to be the religion of Ancient Egypt. Life and Death, Order and Chaos seem to have been worshipped equally; and I, who believe there's a reason for everything, that everything makes sense if one tries hard enough—I believe with equal conviction that reason is an illusion, that nothing *ever* makes sense. I'm afraid I'll lose the past, so I don't throw anything away; so I live in chaos. A visitor once asked if I was planning to take everything with me to the next world.

My real conversion took place when I was thirteen: I lost confidence in religion (I still believed in morality). Later, I believed in art. In Israel, at the Western Wall, I found a surprising residue of feeling for everything I'd been taught to worship as a child.

But in Egypt, something else—something about the relation between how massive these monuments are, how heroic, and how old (older than almost anything else we call art) and fragile. They've been on earth so long, they seem tired of it—tired of time.

They're shrinking by the week, by the hour. On the river bank, at the edge of the mountains and the desert, we tromp over stones and dirt (there's still some sand in my shoes), we lean on columns, pet the sphinxes, rub the giant scarab for luck. They don't resist—they've never resisted—the daily invasion of priests and pilgrims, guards and guides, postcard-sellers and photo-opportunists, righteous gentiles and holocaust victims; each of us taking our little souvenir as we pass through.

They don't look down. Above our human heads, the temples, or what's left of them, are moving into their other life. You can practically hear them slipping away, following those who built them (stumbling over stones, sand in their shoes) and those who had them built: their dust returning eagerly to dust.

Is this the body through which the spirit breathes? My brief Egypt! Graphic close-up of my own dissolution. In this carnival of souls, half marketplace, half theater, in this un-holy land where the spirit sleeps and nothing is not for sale, the spirit wakes, struggling to remain in this world while the beautiful body falls away.

from Little Kisses (2017)

for David Stang

LITTLE KISSES

My mother is mad at the sun.

She hates the daylight—one more new day.

In a nursing home, stuck in a wheelchair, she thinks she's been abandoned.

In the background a woman's nonstop wail—my mother can barely hear me on the phone.

She doesn't know she's speaking to her son.

I have to tell her she's speaking to her son.

"Oh, then I'm not alone! I have a son!"

> *"Please, don't forget that."*

"How could I forget that? . . . and you—who are you?"

*

"Are we related?"

> "Of course."

"Are you my father?"

> "Don't you remember your father?"

"Are you my brother?"

127

"You're my mother."

"I'm your mother?"

"Of course."

"Was I a good mother?"

"You were—you *are*—a wonderful mother."

"I'm glad you're my son. What's your name?"

"You don't remember?"

"I can't think of it—I'm all mixed up . . . Are we related?"

"You're my mother."

"Did I ask you that before?"

"Yes."

"Are you angry?"

"Why should I be angry?"

"Because I'm so stupid."

*

"What lovely flowers," the nurse says, "did your son bring them?"

"Who?"

"Your son. Isn't this your son?"

"He's my friend."

I can't stop myself: "Where is your son?"

"Where's my son? What do you mean?"

"Where is your son now?"

"He's dead."

*

"Mrs. Schwartz, your son is on the phone."

"My son?"

"Yes. Say hello."

"Hello."

"Hello! How are you feeling?"

"Much better, thank you. Why did you call?"

"I call you every day."

"Forgive me, darling. I didn't remember."

*

"Well, *hell*-o! How did you know I was here?

This is my son, isn't that right?

You're my son, aren't you?

You came out of my body. I'm your mother.

Isn't that right?

Isn't he handsome—even if he has a beard.

I'm your mother, I'd love you no matter what you looked like.

Wouldn't I?

> *Gimme a little kiss, will ya huh?*
> *What are ya gonna miss. Will ya huh?*
>
> *Gosh oh gee, why do you refuse?*
> *I can't see whatcha gonna lose.*
>
> *So gimme a little kiss,*
> *Will ya huh?*
>
> *And I'll give it right back to you!*

See, I know all the words!

(I probably won't remember them tomorrow.)"

MY OTHER GRANDMOTHER

Her pale square face looks out like Fate—
through a dark kerchief clipped under her chin

with a narrow, elegant pin; you can make out
a white headband under her shawl; her jacket

and skirt cut from the same coarse dark cloth.
The uneven stitches of her hem hand-sewn—

dark leather men's shoes sticking out.
Yet her face has no coarseness—high cheekbones,

high forehead, small nose. Her narrow, suspicious eyes
don't give much away. The corners of her mouth

turn down almost in a sneer. Her private mind at work.

The closer you look, the younger she seems. Forty
dressed up to look sixty? She could be an actress

in a peasant costume—except for the rough
cloth of her thick hands, her long thick fingers in her lap

curling under her long thumb. Her hips seem broad,
but maybe the thick cloth makes her look heavy.

Her sons and daughters—one greedy; one
resigned to poverty and loose teeth; one fat and jolly; one

angry with the world—unfatherly, unmotherly (yet he could
still charm the ladies)—was it from her they

inherited their bitterness? Their charm? Their nerve?

Her only trace, this worn photo, crudely cut out
and pasted to a piece of cardboard.

My father must have carried it with him. Did he
ever hear a word from her (*could she write?*)—

or about her—after he left home; left Europe?
Did he know when she had died?

Her name was Leah—he never spoke of her.

LOST CAUSES

Jacky Searle (1949–1997)

"You learn so many things in your life," she said the day after she learned the doctors could offer her no further hope—

"but no one teaches you how to die."

Rushing to fill the silence that filled the room, I said: "Don't they say we start learning that the day we're born?"

"Yes," she said, "I suppose that's another way to look at it."

*

"Devoted daughter" and "family rebel" (an only child, like you); "charismatic teacher" and "spiritual conscience" (patron saint: St. Francis); activist; organizer; passionate disapprover of her mother's politics of disapproval—

marathon runner in a hurry to get the operations, radiation, chemotherapy over with and get back to her running—

obstinate optimist (your opposite): your cousin; your "*sister*"—

how old she looks since our last visit—

back in the hospital, her face hollow; the dull yellow skin hanging on her cheekbones; the sharp clear eyes in your early painting of her now also yellow, larger than life but clouded over; her hair grown back, but still short, and suddenly ashen—

she hadn't said much—

we'd been talking about TV shows—

*

"Dear Ms. Searle: I feel extremely lucky to have had you hold my hand and point me in the right direction in life. I remember pushing to sit at your feet at Literature, just for the chance to play with the velcro on your shoes!"

*

At 42, against her mother's reservations, she married an ex-priest ("a foreigner," her mother said, "with black eyes")—then moved into a small house two doors from her mother.

"To keep an eye on her," she said ("*It's a mistake,*" you predicted).

"I've always been partial," she said, "to lost causes."

(She once had a plan to turn the White House into a homeless shelter.)

Two years later, she discovered a tiny lump.

*

"She was my rock. While she was running around trying to figure out how to give more money to one of her causes, I was trying to figure out which movie to go to."

*

After each new piece of bad news, she'd repeat: "The doctors tell me I'm in the best possible position."

She refused to get a second opinion, she explained, "because my doctors would think I didn't trust them" ("*I don't trust doctors,*" you said).

Even after her vital functions began to fail she kept asking for "one more treatment."

Quietly she submitted to a parishioner's idea for a hands-on "healing" ceremony ("*She'll try anything, now*," you said).

*

"*She had expectations not only for herself but for us . . . in a way, we too were first graders.*"

*

In the hospital, at her bedside, her mother and her husband screamed at each other about whether she should have a hospital-bed at home: "*I'm her mother!*" "*But I'm her husband!*"

Months after the funeral her mother still says: "I'll never introduce him as my son-in-law."

On the morning before she lost consciousness for the last time (at home, in a hospital-bed)—

when she finally woke, and her husband asked: "What can I do for you?"—

she signaled him to bend his ear to her mouth and whispered: "*Will you marry me?*"

*

"*When we heard the news about Ms. Searle my girlfriends and I just had to go to the bathroom.*"

*

In the later stages of her disease, she admitted to you (*and to herself?*) how bitterly she resented having to work so hard to stay alive, while "some people" (not saying "*you*") did nothing to take care of themselves.

"She wasn't the person she wanted to be," you said, "but she tried very hard to be the person she wanted to be."

135

*

At 13, she wrote about her private world, her "retreat":

> *The beach at night is a somber place . . . a graveyard filled with the skeletons of the beautiful and the ugly . . . no stars . . . blackness far as I can see . . . a cemetery that changes with every tide . . . yet it creates a peace inside me that I have never known before . . . The blackness hides everything . . . I am free . . . Sometimes I feel that perhaps God created the beach and the night especially for me.*

At 13, she wrote:

> *I shall burst if I become even a little bit happier . . . I take care that my back is always to the world.*

THE CONDUCTOR

Breezing easily between exotic Chinoiserie
and hometown hoedown, whisking lightly between
woodwind delicacy and jazzy trombone, he must have
the widest and oddest repertoire of gestures, which
allows him a stylistic and dynamic range unusual
even among today's most highly regarded conductors.
The way he slipped from the grandiose opening Adagio
maestoso to the suddenly jaunty Allegretto made me
laugh out loud. Though his small, complex gesticulations
can diminish and even undermine the passages
where the melodic lines ought to soar.

He's all dippy knees, flappy elbows, and floppy wrists.
Not Bernstein's exaggerated self-immolation, but
little, complicated pantomimes: steering a car down a
winding road, patting down a mud pie, robbing eggs
from a bird's nest (and carrying them carefully away), flinging
tinsel on a Christmas tree.
                              As a baseball umpire, he could
declare a runner simultaneously safe and out at home plate.

He threw himself into the music—and very nearly into
the first violin section—with the kind of reckless abandon
that comes only with complete confidence and authority;
not so much confidence in himself and authority over
his players, but confidence in his players, and authority
over his material.

These glittering performances: more
dazzle than warmth, more brilliance than magic. Sophistication
without innocence. Does the music ever hold surprises
even for himself? Or terrors?

How much would we love him if it did?

GOLDRING

Getting out of his car one night, he discovers—*No! It's gone!*—the ring he'd worn on his left pinky for more than thirty years.

He treasured it.

Not because an old lover had given it to him—she'd stopped meaning anything to him decades ago.

But because it was an elegant thing: "like gold to airy thinness beat."

The band was etched with delicate crosshatchings—though some of the strokes had worn down to the same smoothness as the inside of the ring.

The part that slid onto—and off—his finger.

It was always a little big for his pinky, so he developed the habit of feeling for the ring with his thumb and pushing it down his finger.

So it would be safe.

He had done this for thirty years.

Why should he lose it now?

*

He'd been having a bad run of luck.

A downward spiral.

Little things.

Like discovering he'd forgotten to record a movie he'd waited years to see—rushing home to see it, but no movie.

He never did that.

An unusual button had popped off his favorite shirt—he put it safely away; but where was it?

Where did it go?

Then while he was inching through a crowded intersection—*BAM!*—a driver who wasn't paying attention slammed into his car.

No one was hurt, thank God.

But he cursed the driver.

And he cursed God.

And now the ring.

He used to feel lucky, but he was beginning to think his luck had changed.

*

He searches around the curb near his car.

He reaches under the driver's seat.

He searches his driveway.

He combs through the trash bag.

He feels under his bed, where that morning he'd tucked in the sheet.

Could it be somewhere in his house, someplace hard to see, a place he hadn't looked?

He sticks his hand down the disposal in his sink.

*

Losing the ring is worse than the car accident.

Much worse.

His finger feels empty.

He feels empty and sad.

One more irreplaceable thing lost.

Another little hole in his life.

He keeps feeling for the ring with his thumb.

*

Endings—separations, partings—always leave him melancholy.

At a party, he's always the last to leave.

Leaving a city he likes, he'll linger on a favorite street corner when he should be packing for the airport.

Or in a museum, looking at a painting he'd come far to see (and might never see again); then peeking back into the room for one last look—then still one more—before finally tearing himself away.

You can't live in a museum.

Or one autumn when the leaves were especially vibrant—crimson and burgundy reflected in an enchanting chain of ponds alongside the road he was driving down (had he ever seen such intense reds?)—he'd have stayed forever; but it was already growing dark, and the leaves would be gone long before he could return.

He has a hard time letting go.

*

This is worse.

He almost asks God to help him find the ring.

Does he really think God can help him find it?

Didn't a missing carton of records turn up a year after he had moved into his new house?

And the book he couldn't find for months?

Even his comfortable shoes (what a thing to misplace!)—they eventually turned up too.

He never stopped looking.

And didn't he thank God when he finally found them?

Or when his father, who couldn't move or speak, died in the hospital the night before his mother was going to take him home?

It would have killed her.

Didn't he thank God for his father's death?

*

So what does he have to lose?

*

But he doesn't ask.

Does he feel foolish?

Or just not want to waste his wish on something unworthy, some material thing, even a thing that was precious to him?

Maybe he hadn't loved the ring enough.

*

He reads elegies—"The art of losing . . . ," "Nothing gold can stay . . ."—but they don't console him.

Maybe he should write his own poem—the way other poets turn their losses into poems.

Wasn't he a writer?

Didn't he need some loss in order to write?

*

But wouldn't writing keep reopening the wound?

The more he wrote, the more he'd miss the ring.

Would he love what he wrote as much as he loved the ring?

143

Would he have to thank God for what he wrote?

Would he have to thank God for losing the ring?

> *

He misses the ring.

He hates God.

He doesn't believe in God.

He tries to write.

He keeps looking.

> *

And what if he found the ring?

CROSSWORD

for David

You're doing a crossword.
I'm working on a puzzle.
Do you love me enough?
What's the missing word?
Do I love you enough?
Where's the missing piece?
Yesterday I was cross with you.
You weren't paying enough attention.
You were cross with me.
I wasn't paying enough attention.
Our words crossed.
Where are the missing pieces?
What are the missing words?
Yet last night we fit together like words in a crossword.
Pieces of a puzzle.

SIX WORDS

yes
no
maybe
sometimes
always
never

Never?
Yes.
Always?
No.
Sometimes?
Maybe—

maybe
never
sometimes.
Yes—
no
always:

always
maybe.
No—
never
yes.
Sometimes,

sometimes
(always)
yes.
Maybe
never . . .
No,

no—
sometimes.
Never.
Always?
Maybe.
Yes—

yes no
maybe sometimes
always never.

IS LIGHT ENOUGH?

Who's there? I can't seem to make out anything or anyone. Is
anyone there? Is that you? In this dim light
that's not light, it's not light enough
to see who's there. I've been waiting for you—asking myself when
you were going to come. Or call. I don't like this
uncertainty, this half-light, this state of bewilderment.
Make it stop. Make it stop before I start crying.
Now I'm shaking, shivering—I want to steady my head against
your chest. Where better to find peace? Wait! I hear your steps—the
sound of your breath, your breathing. Unmistakably yours even in the dark.
Come closer! Find your way into the room. The wind always shuts
the door, so you don't have to. Closer! Sit down
here, near me. Tell me something. Answer me. Is the
light enough? Should I tell you to open or pull down the shades?

NEW NAME

James asked me from now on to call him May—not June.
James May. (He wanted to keep the double stress,
just couldn't stand the endless rhymes with moon
and spoon.) Of course he had his doubts, but not to obsess
over them would be like gardening in Eden without a snake.
In any case, the point now was rendered moot,
since he'd made up his mind to have his cake
and eat it too, and this cake was a beaut—
all icing! Like some rediscovered silent in which Garbo,
like Keaton in *The Playhouse*, chose to play
every part herself: drunk, diva, hooker, housewife, hobo,
queen. And king. The shooting didn't take even a day,
and every costume had a dazzling multi-colored rhinestone
clasp hiding the secret pocket for her favorite cologne.

LA VALSE

Freedom ends or starts with a funeral.
—Frank Bidart

Death sails into the gilded ballroom in purple satin as revealing
as it is liberating—black ostrich plumes at her hip reaching secretly out to
each dancer waltzing by. Long black gloves. What freedom! What the-
ater!—her feathers tickling the legs and rumps of the previously mirthless
company, stuck in their ordinary, unadventurous if not entirely bourgeois
histories. Suddenly, the whole room comes alive. Everyone feels it, that
instant exhilaration, relaxation, absence of tension and fear; the muscles in their
faces relocating into smiles, their breaths exhaling sighs of pleasure, their daily
rhythms revised. Isn't she, at this moment, a work of art? Lifting lives
out of the commonplace, offering all-too-rare possibilities, insights. Are
we grateful to have this moment of intensity, of momentary pleasure (grazed
by the pain of its very momentariness)? How swiftly she swirls by
us. How easily the dance changes color. How eagerly we flee these enchanting
dancers for the usual warmongers, pickpockets, and enchanting murderers.

TEHRAN SPRING

by Affonso Romano de Sant'Anna

ON THE ROOFTOPS OF IRAN

Over the starlit rooftops, in Iran,
echoes the agonized voice
                        of those who only want
to say something.

Not the litany of the muezzins
and their monotonous prayers,

asking no questions, insisting on the same answers.

It's the green song tearing
off the black cloth of the ayatollahs
as if from high above the houses
it would be possible to anticipate
                        the birth of light
that bloodies the dawn.

ZAYANDE ("THE ONE WHO GIVES LIFE")

In Iran there's a river
that comes down from the mountains
with no desire whatsoever
to throw itself into the sea.

It prefers to go to go to go
nowhere
without explaining
its motives for moving.

It races past us
on its travels,
its departure part
of its own brief arrivals.

Like a rushing train,
that makes a home
of each station it passes:
it moves on; it remains.

Transitive verb of being:
to be
is both the being
and the what's-going-to-be.

Lovers families children flowers
have all testified:
the river stays in their lives
never intending to stay.

Where it came
from, it knows,
and knows where it
wants to go.

Though it starts high among the snow-caps,
its ocean is the desert,
and what's waiting for it
         are whitecaps of sand,
         shoals of hard rock
         and bitter earth-apples
         covered with the grit
of a bitter underground sea.

To meet its destiny,
         this river,
                  saint-like,
has taken its name
from its harshest surroundings—
stripping itself
of the anxiety
other rivers have
as they daydream
of joining the sea,
—giving up everything
to be fried
in the desert's pure flame.

When others find its path strange,
and go rattling on
about the marvels of the sea,
the river will whisper
to its fishes: Listen—
the desert is my other half.

Who wants to be
just another river
dribbling into the sea?
What a dull way for a river
to achieve glory.
The ocean, I know,
would take me in. But my fate
is this:
          to live within my own limits;
and to make the desert come alive.

It is written into my name.

TEHRAN SPRING

This spring there's still snow
in the mountains circling Tehran
but the thaw has already begun.

Although women are wearing their black chadors,
suddenly you can see patterns of embroidery over the dark background,
a variety of colors springing up on the most daring outfits,
and at any moment
                     from some black caterpillar
a chrysalis will appear,
suddenly one can predict the flight of butterflies.

SMALL AIRPORT IN BRAZIL

9:31 in the departure lounge, nearly
deserted. Monday night—everyone here

is a little too tired to be traveling
to another city. I search for an interesting face

behind the newspapers, and light on
a young man:

maybe 31?—slim and well-dressed (that is,
dressed with some thought): his tan

jacket and pressed gray pants in muted
harmony with a pale yellow shirt

open at the collar (no tie, though there may
have been one earlier).

They fit him elegantly, suit him, suit
his thin, sandy hair and pale,

fair skin. His rimless glasses suggest
seriousness not fashion: a tone

confirmed by the forward gaze behind them—
through them.

He wears a touchingly simple
gold band on his finger, another example

of natural elegance—his wife must
share his taste.

Is he on his way to her? Is she picking him up
at another small airport? Will they embrace

warmly, gracefully, when he arrives?
Or will she be up waiting for him at home, dinner

on the table? Or not—already asleep
when he finally gets in, after her own long day.

Or is he on his way to yet another hotel,
after a week of hotels?

—tired of hotels; while his attractive,
witty, attentive wife, with her eloquent cheekbones

and slightly sunken cheeks,
begins to show her own weariness of

spending so many nights alone.

They'll cost something, these nights.
Everything costs something when you have to make

your way through the world—
even if you're not new to the idea,

or just beginning
not to be new to it.

IN FLIGHT

"Did you hear what I was playing, Lane?"
"I didn't think it polite to listen, sir."
—*The Importance of Being Earnest*

A big, hefty guy next to me, an even bigger guy
already squeezed into the window seat. Big, pleasant
fellows. Strangers before this three-hour nonstop

domestic flight. But they've been talking away nonstop
since before takeoff. Talking business. Talking sports.
China. India (my next-seat neighbor might have been

from India). Talking Cubs and Red Sox (they both love
them both). Google. The Euro. Leverage. Banks. Bailouts.
Masters of Money ("It will change the way you think").

Great deals and missed opportunities. Exxon. Fracking.
Megabus. Amtrak. Breakdowns. Lost luggage and
missed connections. A good place to stay in Detroit.

Neither Cheez-Its nor Diet Cokes inhibit the juggernaut.

So much experience, so many theories, so much
friendly advice. The urgent need to tell each other
everything they know before the flight is over—

the Indian fellow occasionally bumping my left arm
in his enthusiasm. "Exactly!" "Absolutely!"
All they've learned and thought, pouring out.

Pouring out, yet steering clear of delicate subjects: politics
(they know better than that), or home (an hour into the flight,
"my wife" has become "ex-wife"). No names.

Nothing about movies or television. No mention of
any other book. No music. But thoroughly tuned in
to each other ("Exactly!" "Absolutely!"),

handing over and taking in
whatever they can in 195 minutes—
like old friends.

Except not.

As we begin our rough descent, a startling
silence fills the cabin. One of them has drifted
into sleep. Stretching to look out the window

I can make out farmland, roads, then tractors,
and cars. Some bumps, and the sleeper awakes.
But the conversation is over. Shutting down.

Touching down. Each of us left with our own thoughts
of arrival or another departure. Then the busy powering up
of phones, the clumsy lowering of overhead bags.

Jamming the aisle, eager to get off and on
with our lives. No handshakes. No goodbyes. But
separated in the crowd, and each with a little wave,

they call out. "Sam." "Andy."

TO MY OLDEST FRIEND, WHOSE
SILENCE IS LIKE A DEATH

In today's paper, a story about our high school drama
teacher evicted from his Carnegie Hall rooftop apartment

made me ache to call you—the only person I know
who'd still remember his talent, his good looks, his self-

absorption. We'd laugh (at what haven't we laughed?), then
not laugh, wondering what became of him. But I can't call,

because I don't know what became of you.

—After sixty years, with no explanation, you're suddenly
not there. Gone. Phone disconnected. I was afraid

you might be dead. But you're not dead.

You've left, your landlord says. He has your new unlisted
number but insists on "respecting your privacy." I located

your oldest son, who refuses to tell me anything except that
you're alive and not ill. Your ex-wife ignores my letters.

What's happened? Are you in trouble? Something
you've done? Something *I've* done?

We used to tell each other everything: our automatic
reference points to childhood pranks, secret codes,

and sexual experiments. How many decades since we started
singing each other "Happy Birthday" every birthday?

(Your last uninhibited rendition is still on my voice mail.)

How often have we exchanged our mutual gratitude—the easy
unthinking kindnesses of long friendship.

This mysterious silence isn't kind. It keeps me
up at night, bewildered, at some "stage" of grief.

Would your actual death be easier to bear?

I crave your laugh, your quirky takes, your latest
comedy of errors. "When one's friends hate each other,"

Pound wrote near the end of his life, "how can there be
peace in the world?" We loved each other. Why why why

am I dead to you?

Our birthdays are looming. The older I get, the less and less
I understand this world,

and the people in it.

JERRY GARCIA IN A SOMERVILLE PARKING LOT

Past midnight, a man in his late 60s, tall, with long
gray hair and a bushy gray (almost white) beard,
returns to the side street public parking lot
where he'd left his car. It's hot, and dark, and the lot
is unlit. At the far end he can make out two men
smoking, leaning against the car right next to his.

Alone and apprehensive, he starts across the lot, and
soon catches a whiff of what they're smoking.
Suddenly one of them asks:

"Want to hear a joke?"

Startled, he hesitates, but obliges. "Sure," he says.
"What's the joke?" "OK: What do you call a woman

with only one leg?" "I don't know," he plays along.
"What do you call a woman with only one leg?"

"Eileen."

It takes him a second, he almost groans, and then
begins to laugh.

"Want a drag?" the guy asks. He's just a kid
(the other one never says a word). "No, no thanks,"
the man answers, "I can inhale from here."

This time it's the kid who laughs. "OK. I only asked
because you look like Jerry Garcia.

—Have a nice night!"

"You too," the man answers, unlocking his car.
"Thanks." And all the way home, he keeps chuckling
at lucky escapes, wildly mistaken identities, sweet

dumb jokes (how little it takes to restore his
affection for the city), and at least for the moment
gratefully alive, can't stop laughing—or laughing at

himself for laughing—at his latest temporary reprieve.

New Poems (2001–2021)

VERMEER'S PEARL

I used to boast that I never lived in a city without a Vermeer.

—You do now, a friend pointed out, when the one Vermeer in my city was stolen.

It's still missing.

The museum displays its empty frame.

But there are eight Vermeers in New York, more than any other city—and not so far away.

Sometimes even more.

Once, the visiting Vermeer was one of his most beloved paintings.

It was even more beautiful than I remembered.

A young girl, wearing a turban of blue and yellow silk, is just turning her face to watch you entering the room.

She seems slightly distracted by someone a little off to your right, maybe someone she knows better than you.

Her mouth is slightly open, as if she's just taken a breath and is about to speak.

The light falling on her is reflected not only on her large pearl earring but also in her large shining eyes ("Those are pearls," sings Ariel of a man drowned in a tempest at sea, "that were his eyes").

167

And on her moist lips.

There's even a little spot of moisture in a corner of her mouth.

Some art historians think this was not intended to be a portrait, just a study of a figure in an exotic costume.

Yet her presence is so palpable, she seems right there in the room with you, radiating unique and individual life.

Already in the museum is another Vermeer in which a woman writing a letter has a similar pearl earring.

She's interrupted by her maid handing her a letter—is it from the person she's just been writing to?

And in a nearby museum there's a painting of a young woman with piercing eyes and another enormous pearl dangling from her ear (a "teardrop pearl").

She's staring out a window and tuning a lute.

Scholars tell us that these pearls aren't really pearls—no pearl so large has ever come to light.

No oyster could be big enough.

So the famous pearl is probably just glass painted to look like a pearl.

Pearl of no price.

Yet as you look, the illusion of the pearl—the *painted* pearl, glistening, radiant, fragile, but made real by the light it radiates—becomes before your eyes a metaphor for the girl wearing it.

Or if not the girl, then Vermeer's painting of her.

ESCHER: *STILL LIFE WITH MIRROR* (1934)

Look into the tilted mirror. You can't see your face, just
the reflection of a toothbrush and toothpaste (*PIM*)
standing in a water glass, the back of a saint's card tucked
into the corner: Anthony carrying the Holy Child. A basket
with an unwieldy sponge hangs by strings looped over one post
of the mirror-stand. Wedged under one edge, a little tin—
"SKIN FOOD"—keeps the mirror askew. On the dressing table, not
reflected, a guttered candle, perfume (*My Sin?*), a comb in a hairbrush,
all resting on a white doily with lace trim. But in the mirror—
something uncanny—not, as I said, your face, but a narrow
arched street, with black doorways and windows receding
into the future, luring us away from our preparations
to meet the world, into a world inviting yet closed
to us—sinister wonderland hopeless to resist.

THE WORLD

(from the tarot deck)

Let's begin in the beginning, or at the end—aren't they really
the same? *Creation/Revelation.* A snake chewing its own tail,
circumscribing a naked lady clutching stiff twin staffs, like giant
pencils (to scribble whose long story?). Glazed trophy heads—a dazed
(or dazzled?) lion, a blowhard bull, a glaring eagle, and one benign
human face—surround her; sounding her, staring her down. But stark naked,

she has arisen, and she's stepping out.

Off to her writing desk? Her raven? Her haven? Do revelations lie
in store? Is this how she conceives *The World*? The round earth's
imagined corners: trumpets, strumpets, numberless infinities;
demons mangled, angels strangled, angles tangled; from lowly
ground, forms arising, dissolving; from dearth: hearth, birth; then—*burn,
batter, blow*—death, woe (with every grace, abundant tyrannies).

Look, daybreak again—or twilight. *The snake bites!* Repent. Pardon. Mourn.

GOD HOUR (ERIC LUNDQUIST: IN MEMORIAM)

"Eric McNeil Lundquist, born on December 15, 1959, died at age 58 on August 14, 2018. He attended Massachusetts College of Art and lived in Dorchester for 30 years. Despite a lifelong struggle with bipolar disorder, Eric was a talented artist and spiritual person. He had many good friends, loved seventies music, ran four Boston marathons, and was an avid collector of Superman memorabilia. A memorial service is planned."

YES . . . I am still very diligently meditating on the TRANSCENDENTAL. I enter my "large closet" and sit in total darkness except for the illuminated screen of the iPad. Incense fills my nostrils. I have spent countless hours engaged in meditation on the TRANSCENDENTAL over the last 34 years. Nothing . . . nothing brings me greater joy. My spirit flies free. Do other people ever experience this exalted state? As I sit out my allotted time meditating in the closet I sit with folded hands and bow in reverence.

*

THE ABSOLUTE

No mind, no form, I only exist;
  Now ceased all will and thought.
The final end of Nature's dance,
  I am It whom I have sought.

A realm of Bliss bare, ultimate;
  Beyond both Knower and Known;

A rest immense I enjoy at last;
  I face the One alone . . .

My spirit aware of all the heights,
  I am mute in the core of the Sun.
I barter nothing with time and deeds;
  My cosmic play is done.

                    —Sri Chinmoy

It took me a very long time to memorize this poem.

                    *

Everything I'm doing with regards to meditation is an earnest effort to prepare myself for the time of death. Decade after decade . . . Minute after minute . . . I have in the past and will proceed in the future to embark on the greatest of any journey imaginable.

                    *

The focus of my attention is "between the eyebrows and a little above." As I gaze I say, "I am throwing everything into the ever transcending beyond." Then, one by one, I imagine myself throwing all the people in my life into a spiritual bath in which they are scrubbed clean of all impurities.

I feel I'm "drilling myself into a liberated soul."

"Infinity itself" is a place of such comfort.

I've begun to live my life free of normal daily concerns. It's as if nothing and no-one exists.

I don't believe I will ever die.

                    *

I hold the speaker of my little tape player over my heart. I can feel my heart percolating. This practice means more to me now than ever before. I know . . . I know . . . so many times in the past I've sworn I'd give it up. But every single time I do, I'm reminded of how important it has become.

*

TO WHOM IT MAY CONCERN, ERIC MCNEIL LUNDQUIST IS CURRENTLY INDULGING IN THE ACTIVITY OF RITUALIZED MEDITATION ON THE TRANSCENDENTAL PHOTOGRAPH OF SRI CHINMOY. IT IS A POSITIVE HABIT THAT IS SO DEEPLY IN-GRAINED THAT HE COULDN'T KEEP FROM ENGAGING IN IT EVEN IF HE WANTED TO.

*

We live in the realm of the relative, unlike god who resides in the realm of the absolute. In the relative (the physical 3-dimensional world) things exist with their polar opposites (fat, thin—inside, outside—up, down—male, fe-male . . .). Whereas in the realm of the absolute all of the differences have been reconciled. We all exist in the realm of the relative while living and then enter into the realm of the absolute when we "die." But we never "die"—only change from one form to another in an endless cycle from form to spirit and then back again, constantly making progress.

*

Okay!! . . . Here we go . . . (cup of "java" in hand) . . . Today it is in the early morning hours on September 29th, 2012, and as I am comfortably situated within the coziness of the sacred-safe-haven, the magical melodies of the seven-ties are caressing my eardrums. *"Can music save your mortal soul?"* Even now as I write this g-mail, I find myself being hurled headlong into a realm of ecstatic bliss and harmony.

I'm so used to the vibrations of the subway that I've become totally oblivious.

I spend so much time listening to popular music because I very much believe that constantly exposing oneself to its upbeat messages will drive positivity deeply into the core of consciousness.

*

I AM CURRENTY RESIDING QUITE COMFORTABLY WITHIN THE SECLUDED CONFINES OF THE AMAZING, FABULOUS, TERRIFIC, EXTRA-ORDINARY, STUPENDOUS, SUPERB, FAN-TASTIC, WONDERFUL, REMARKABLE, FANTASMAGORACAL... SACRED-SAFE-HAVEN ... (FORMERLY "THE SANCTUARY-ECSTASY-ABODE" AND LATER "THE OASIS-EUPHORIA-REFUGE")... GROOVIN' TO THE MUSIC OF THE SIXTIES AND SEVENTIES... WHICH IS CATAPULTING MY INNER SPIRITUAL BEING HEAD OVER HEELS INTO THE FURTHEST FLUNG RE-GIONS OF ECSTATIC, ELATED, EXPANSIVE, ULTIMATE, FAR-REACHING AND VOLCANICALLY ERUPTIVE TRANSCENDEN-TAL CONSCIOUSNESS.

WHEW! I AM WORN OUT!!

*

The "GOD-HOUR" is between 3:00am and 4:00am. This morning (since I got a good night's sleep) I was able to rise at the god-hour and enter very ef-fortlessly into meditation.

*

I have eight albums by Akasha. They are: SKY WINGS ... LIFE SONG ... DELIGHT ... NEW DAWN ... IN THE COSMIC FLOW ... IN THE VERY DEPTHS OF MY ASPIRATION HEART ... BLUE HORIZON ... FOUNTAIN OF JOY and one more that I have yet to get called DREAM GLOW. I totally, completely and thoroughly love every one of the songs on all of these albums.

The instrument I'm most fond of is called "the esraj."

*

At the start of each weekly meditation meeting we'd do a silent meditation and then very soulfully sing the invocation. It only took a short time to learn all the words and then I sang right along with all the others.

Unfortunately I was unable to continue with the group. For the next ten years I was in and out of mental hospitals. It made continuing with meditation impossible. It wasn't until several years later that I branched out on my own path (alone without the group). Those were difficult years but all the way along I continued with my meditational practices.

*

Never in a million years did I imagine I'd continue to meditate for so long. Who would have guessed I'd get such a big kick out of sitting motionless for endless hours listening to a Swedish women's singing group and gaping at the photograph of a man whom I consider to be my "spiritual master." When I was a teenager the word meditation wasn't even in my vocabulary. Whoda-thunk-it?

*

I'm definitely back into the great feelings of elation that I've become so accustomed to experiencing. NEVER!! . . . NEVER!! . . . NEVER!! again will I speak ill of Sri Chinmoy. It is directly due to him that I so delightfully live the spiritual life every day. My ritual has turned into a healthy obsession that continues to give me the conviction that GOD EXISTS in my life. I WILL do it until the day I die.

*

I know I've said it before but I'm going to state it again: The reason I spend such an enormous amount of time in deep meditation is because I'm preparing my soul for "swift passage at the time of death." My most closely held beliefs are the ones that will follow me at the time of "crossing over." I aspire to realize

God in this life-time so that I won't have to reincarnate and live another life. But I'm having a tremendous load of fun this time around, if I have to come back, I'd love to do it all over again.

*

You probably think I'm nuts the way I carry on about spirituality and medi-tation. I can't help it. . . . even after all these years I'm more jazzed than ever.

*

Here are details about the meeting yesterday with the oncologist. Eric asked a few questions, but the doctor tended to use medical terminology and I think his abil-ity to get what she was saying was limited. She was thorough though, and I was pleased with her expertise. Mary, Jane, and I are working on putting the points below in words that are clearer to Eric.

1. The diagnosis is either pancreatic cancer or cholangiocarcinoma, which is can-cer of the bile ducts. Neither is curable.

2. With either one the prognosis is poor.

3. He will get the cyber knife treatment next week. It is a single focused dose of radiation to the one lesion in the brain to prevent neurologic complications— limb paralysis, seizure, speech difficulty, altered level of consciousness. I am glad Eric is willing to go ahead with it. Side effects should be minimal to none.

4. There is no surgical option.

5. Chemotherapy might prolong his life 3 to 6 months. Eric is currently opposed to it. Neither I nor the doctor tried to persuade him to reconsider. He indicates that his wish is to have quality of life rather than quantity of life. We and the doctors have all made sure that he understands that the choices regarding treat-ment are up to him. To him quality means closeness of family and friends. Also the ability to maintain his meditation practice.

6. He repeats that he does not fear death, but having had significant pain recently, he does want adequate pain control. I will send a separate email regarding adequate pain management.

7. He is in good spirits, but may be in denial.

I will try to answer any questions you may have—call, text, email.

*

"I live so much in the moment," he told me, "I can't imagine dying."

*

"I know my family and my friends are going to have to deal with my loss. But I don't have to."

*

"I'm so happy I'll be seeing my mother before anyone else. And even if that's not true I can believe it if I want to."

*

"No Price Is Too Great To Pay For Inner Peace."

HARVEST

A man in a tree, upside down, hanging by his legs, shaking down pears.

A peasant spread-eagled under a tree—mouth open, snoring, his codpiece loosened, his 400-year-old cap so thinly painted you can see right through it.

Also under that tree, eight field workers—male and female, young and old, well-fed and rail-thin—munching, sipping, slurping, guzzling, gobbling their noon repast: cheese, porridge, gruel, wine; with a large knife, one carves off a slice of bread from a loaf in a basket.

Mowers.

Gleaners.

Fruit-gatherers.

Scythes sharpened daily.

A distant team of oxen hauling into town a wagon heavy with a barn-size load of wheat.

Wheat.

Fields of wheat.

Hills of wheat.

Distant wheat.

Narrow paths in the wheat.

Two women bearing sheaves on their shoulders and a third—their heads poking out above a narrow path in the wheat.

A man lugging two heavy jugs emerging from a narrow path in the wheat.

Endless wheat.

Bloody games on the village green.

Villagers or field workers swimming—or bathing?—in a pond.

Cows grazing.

Thatched roofs sloping nearly to the ground.

Gables of the village church, uphill from the water's edge, nearly hidden behind the trees.

Matchstick ships entering and leaving the harbor.

Gray horizon dissolving into the distance, disappearing into the misty distance.

Two birds taking flight, ascending from the wheat.

A man hanging upside down from a tree.

A peasant spread-eagled under a tree, see-through cap and loosened codpiece—mouth open, snoring.

A pitchfork leaning against the tree.

Resting against the tree.

IN EMILY DICKINSON'S BEDROOM

A chilly light pervades the empty room
bringing neither its current nor former inhabitant peace.
Rather, its immaterial lingering infests
both the air inside and what we see of the grass
outside—brittle, brown, as if it wanted to avoid the sun.
Inside, the visitor must be respectful
and polite, evasive without actually telling lies.
Everything here seems hidden—*is* hidden—not
just the bricked-up chimney and plastered-over doorway. Any
clue—under the wide floorboards, behind the blocked entrance—
to the haunted chambers of a heart? Patches of verse, of
old wallpaper, the main street not yet a street. What industry
motivated those uncanny dashes—these shadows
still eluding our meager efforts to scrutinize.

MY DOCTOR'S DEATH

George Burns, at 99, puffing on his cigar, confided to us
That his doctor had warned him to stop smoking—then noted
That his doctor had died many years ago. Probably
Not a bad doctor. For many years, I had a great doctor.

Someone I could count on not only for my physical
Health, but for my general well-being. I could tell him
Anything—*everything*—and he'd listen, always knowing
Just what to prescribe—and not just medications.

A few years ago he retired. He was ready. It seemed
The right time. I missed him. But of course I knew I wasn't
The only patient he treated with such thoughtfulness.
He deserved a rest from those—from *all* those—obligations,

Those loyalties. He'd earned it. And then the other day,
I heard that he had died. A fast-moving and devastating
Disease, causing him great pain. No doctor could
Stop it. He deserved a long and happy retirement.

He'd earned it.

We say: Physician, heal thyself. But isn't that
Just irony? Who can prevent his own disease?
We know. *We know.* But the mystery remains.
"I told the doctor I broke my leg in two places" (my doctor

Liked Henny Youngman). *"He told me to quit going
To those places."* And Irving Berlin: *"What'll I do
When you are far away and I am blue—what'll I do?"*
Doctors aren't supposed to die. How could he die?

LUBITSCH'S *ANGEL*

It may be hard to remember, but there was once a time when Hollywood (or some people in Hollywood) could take for granted from the audience a certain level of cultural knowledge.

Art. Literature. Classical music.

Take a film called *Angel*, directed in 1937 by Ernst Lubitsch, much admired for his inimitable "touch"—a film now mostly overlooked.

The glamorous heroine, Marlene Dietrich, is married to a British diplomat (the touchingly stolid Herbert Marshall) who devotes more time to the League of Nations than to his attractive wife.

She loves him, but she's frustrated by how much his desire to save the world has blinded him to his need to save their marriage.

So she slips off to Paris to re-visit a social club where she was once, before her marriage, a particularly social member.

On this impulsive visit, she meets dashing Melvyn Douglas, who instantly falls for her.

Hard.

He thinks she's royalty.

He wants to see her again.

That night!

"9:00 o'clock," she tells him.

"8:30," he pleads.

She shakes her head: "9:00 o'clock."

"But your highness," he protests.

"Oh, by the way," she admits, "I'm not the grand duchess . . . quarter-to-nine."

She never tells him her name.

He calls her "Angel."

Frightened by the intensity of this fling, Dietrich returns to London without saying goodbye.

Still searching for her, Douglas crosses paths with Marshall, with whom, during the war, he shared a "seamstress."

He tells Marshall about his "Angel."

Marshall, though disapproving, invites him home to meet his wife.

That night, preparing to attend the opera, Marshall tells Dietrich about meeting Douglas and his friend's irrational infatuation—arousing Dietrich's more than casual interest.

At the opera: Dietrich and Marshall in their box—the camera focusing only on them.

The lights dim.

The opening chords—then fade to black.

Without ever mentioning the title of the opera, Lubitsch assumes we will recognize those familiar chords.

It's Wagner—*Tristan*, in which the trusted young emissary of the Cornish king and the king's bride-to-be fall tragically in love.

It's music's darkest depiction of a love triangle: older man; beautiful wife; dashing young suitor.

Sound familiar?

In the opera, those chords won't be resolved until five hours later, with the death of the lovers, their so-called "Love-Death."

Lubitsch's glancing reference to Wagner is a sardonic yet ominous foreshadowing of the clouds that will in the film increasingly darken our expectation of a happy ending.

He clouds our sense of what a happy ending could be.

And given the surprising emotional depths into which Lubitsch plunges his characters, a happy ending suddenly seems virtually impossible—although knowing Lubitsch, we suspect he won't go so far as to end this movie with a "Liebestod."

The amusing contrivances of plot, and the superb acting he elicits from his stars, make Lubitsch a great director.

But he also expected his audience to understand his allusion.

That dark, knowing little joke.

That little quotation—those four famous chords from the prelude to *Tristan*.

They last only a few seconds.

"The Lubitsch touch."

Lacking this knowledge won't ruin the movie.

But doesn't some cultural understanding add a rich—a *richer*—layer of parallels and alternatives?

Isn't the elaborate care with which Lubitsch sets up and then throws away these few telling seconds the true—maybe even the major—signature of his elusive genius?

RALPH HAMILTON'S FACES

> *. . . at the end of each century, Boston has had a portrait painter of great interpretive gifts—Copley in the 18th, Sargent in the 19th, and, I'd argue, Hamilton in the 20th. . . . He is creating one of those invaluable records that tell what a historical period was about.*
>
> —David Bonetti, *The Boston Phoenix*

"What the hell *is* this," Bea Arthur bellowed, when he shoved his camera up against her nose, "an ad for facial hair?"

He always painted his portraits from his own pictures.

Twenty clicks. Thirty clicks. The eventual photos largely unrecognizable.

> *Pierre Boulez. Sarah Caldwell. Jay Cantor. Elliott Carter. Alfred Chandler. Fay Chandler. Phyllis Curtin. Elsa Dorfman. Richard Dyer.*

If he was lucky, he'd find one shot that worked.

Then he'd project that photo onto a 30-by-30-inch museum-board—filling the entire space with the one face.

> *Annie Fischer. Bob Garis. Bob Ginsberg with his eyes closed. Terry Gross. John Harbison. Seamus Heaney. Rachel Jacoff, her face a lunar landscape. Rudy Kikel. Alice Mattison. Michael Mazur. James Merrill.*

Tracing the contours of that face, he'd turn the projection into a kind of topographical map—readable only to him.

Then, very carefully, he'd fill in all the spaces.

He called this his "paint-by-numbers" phase.

Alice Methfessel. Mark Morris. Seiji Ozawa. Robert Polito. Anja Silja. Harvey Silverglate. Isaac Silverglate. Craig Smith. Jean Stapleton.

Once every space was painted in, he'd take a clean brush and start to move the paint!

To brush the paint away.

Turn the board sideways, then upside down, and keep brushing—brushing and brushing the paint violently away.

"His brushing," one critic wrote, "brings the viewer into direct contact not so much with the illusion of movement as with the inner workings of movement itself."

Stop too soon, the person might not yet have begun to breathe; take too long, the person could get brushed completely away.

High-wire act over an abyss.

Until suddenly that huge face became the face he saw in his head.

Bewildered Klaus Tennstedt. Glamorous Violette Verdy. Michael York.

York, always prepared to be photographed, would "freeze" a split-second ahead of every camera click—and ended up as two separate portraits: each one totally different, each one completely himself.

A hundred faces: Nancy Armstrong to Ben Zander. Comic and tragic masks. Unmasked. The web of our life.

Actors, musicians, writers, dancers, other artists and museum curators.

My father. My mother. John Pijewski's mother.

Himself.

Each face emerging from—emerging from *under*—that volatile surface.

"Looking at a Hamilton portrait," a viewer observed, "is like being in the middle of an intimate conversation."

Each blurring brushstroke an increasingly complex disclosure of tenderness or reproof, curiosity or indifference.

No one he particularly needed to speak to; only someone he needed to speak to him.

TITIAN'S *MARSYAS*

The 16th-century Venetian master's very last painting—as big as life—is the story of the pan-piping satyr who dared to challenge a god.

Titian painted his crucifixion.

He hangs by his ankles from the branches of a tree, his goat-legs askew, as Apollo, kneeling, tenderly skins him alive.

Upside down, his tormented expression reads like a smile.

A thirsty pup is lapping up his blood.

Seated close—rapt—old King Midas, with his golden coronet, contemplates the horrific scene.

It's the 90-year-old artist's self-portrait.

Someone who's learned the cost of making art, the cost of challenging the gods.

And has accepted it.

Except for the glittering crown, most of the surface is rougher, murkier than the master's earlier dazzle.

Close inspection reveals paint smeared by his own fingers.

He put his whole body into this painting.

It was found in his studio after his death.

After how many years could anything still have been left for him to do?

A work is complete, Rembrandt said, if in it the master's intentions have been realized.

THE REHEARSAL

from John Harbison's What Do We Make of Bach?

"At our first duo rehearsal—Bach's B-
Minor Sonata was what we played—I already knew
This young woman interested me.

We borrowed a room (where was it?)
With a harpsichord (whose?)
And with few words began the sonata.

As this unfolded—recognition, confirmation,
Accord, consternation. Above all,
The marking of a common center.

She had told me Bach was her favorite composer,
Her home site, but by the end of the first movement,
I knew that in her case, this was not just

Devotion to the music, its spirit, its
Generosity, but a trust in it,
A willingness to let it speak.

What I heard at the same time, in that
First movement, is the loneliness that often inhabits
The undertone of a great master's work—

The habitation of a realm so rarely visited,
With so little company, to find that secret
In music, the performer needs an inner life,

A kind of solitary experience. I sensed a person

For whom art costs too much, for whom
The sharing of that intense experience
With others is often painful and risky.

I knew what that might be like!

I sensed joy, possibility, danger,
Complication. Inextricability.
A fulcrum. A magnet. A talisman . . .

We began the second movement."

ASTRONOMER

"What's your favorite part of the painting?" the young woman standing next to me suddenly asks.

I reply instantly: "The light hitting the fingernail of the Astronomer's left index finger—what's yours?"

"The edge of his white shirt sticking out from under his sleeve."

Her favorite detail is barely inches away from mine, but we confess that neither of us had paid much attention to the other's choice.

A few minutes later, I might have chosen something else.

*

The Astronomer ranks only 23rd in popularity among Vermeer's 37 extant paintings, although Vermeer himself seems to have been particularly pleased with it.

He both dated it (rare for him) and signed it with his efficiently witty monogram: IVMeer—the V overlapping the central part of the M, the I (for Iohannes) like a tree springing up in the middle of the V.

Two centuries later, it was acquired by the Rothschilds, and after the war, after the "Monuments Men" recovered it from its Nazi hideout (evidently *der Führer* liked it too), the family surrendered it to the Louvre.

*

A man in a dark silk Japanese robe leans over a table cluttered with books, some crumpled notes, an astrolabe, with which medieval navigators calculated the altitude of the stars, and a celestial globe swirling with serpentine constellations.

He's an astronomer.

One book, an old treatise on astronomy and geography (second edition, 1621—the painting is that precise), is open to the chapter recommending both "the aid of mechanical instruments" and "inspiration from God."

Light floods in through a double window, illuminating the book, the globe, the Astronomer's face.

He's leaning so far forward in his chair, he's practically levitating with curiosity.

Like so many of Vermeer's figures, he has a particular look of attentive concentration that suggests an interior life, a private zone of contemplation—yet not self-absorbed.

He touches the globe with the tips of his thumb and middle finger of his right hand—maybe just about to rotate it.

On the wall behind him hangs a dim painting of the finding of Moses in the bulrushes.

*

A long-held but unproven theory suggests that the model for both *The Astronomer* and its companion piece, *The Geographer*, is the Dutch lens-maker and inventor of microbiology Antonie van Leeuwenhoek.

Both he and Vermeer were born and baptized in Delft in 1632.

Forty-three years later, the great scientist was the executor designated to dispose of the property of the recently deceased and indigent artist.

Vermeer might have used his lenses to help create his almost photographic images.

This picture shows someone enthralled with discovery.

Maybe it's a self-portrait.

*

Gradually, the hidden geometry of the painting reveals itself.

So many Vermeers, like *The Woman in Blue Reading a Letter*, or *The Geographer*, are images of stability—solid, unshakable, earthbound.

The pregnant woman in blue looms like the Great Pyramid above the familiar objects in her room that seem to gather around her.

But in *The Astronomer*, the pyramid has been tipped over onto its side, forming an acute angle.

Like the profile of an open eye.

That eye is everywhere.

In the angle of the two fingers touching the globe.

In the angle of the Astronomer's arms—his left hand gripping the edge of the table (steadying him, grounding him), while his right arm reaches out to the celestial globe.

Even in the overlapping shadows cast by the light through the double windows.

Light that catches both the tip of his finger and the edge of his white shirt.

The table, the book, the globe, the Astronomer's body—everything in the process of opening outward and letting in the light.

The whole painting has become an eye.

*

The Astronomer's unembarrassed, open face, luminous even in profile.

His long hair falling below his shoulders, revealing an earring.

Vermeer regards him as lovingly as the Astronomer regards his globe.

Right next to the Astronomer's right hand, the hand beginning to turn the celestial globe, the artist has placed his signature.

NOTES

"Escher: *Still Life with Mirror* (1934)": Commissioned as label copy for *M.C. Escher: Infinite Dimensions*, Boston Museum of Fine Arts, 2018.

"Is Light Enough?": The fourteen end words form a line from Gwendolyn Brooks's "garbageman: the man with the orderly mind." The form, introduced by Terrance Hayes as a tribute to Brooks, is called "The Golden Shovel."

"New Name": *Court Green* challenged poets to write a Bouts-Rimés sonnet with these given end words.

"La Valse": The end words form a sentence from Jean Genet's *Our Lady of the Flowers*.

Affonso Romano de Sant'Anna's "On the Rooftops of Iran" and "Zayande" were translated with the help of Rogério Zola Santiago.

"In Emily Dickinson's Bedroom": In the spring of 2014, the Emily Dickinson Museum invited a number of poets to each spend an hour in her bedroom, which was being restored and not open to the public. The room was empty, with only a chair and little writing desk, on which a tiny basket held a facsimile draft of Dickinson's "A chilly Peace infests the Grass." The visitors were encouraged to write a poem inspired by this experience. This sonnet incorporates every word in the first stanza of Dickinson's poem.